OLD GOLD

A SEASON WITH
CARMARTHEN TOWN

Chris Harte

sports history publishing

First published in Wales in 2013
by Sports History Publishing
Braemar House
Carmarthen, SA31 3DN.
(Tel: 075-8300-0639)

ISBN : 978-1-898010-06-7

Editor : Susan Lewis

Assistant Editor : Lizzie Mead

Cover : Carmarthen Town Football Club

Cover design & layout : Sarah Evans www.sarahlouisedesigns.co.uk

Printed and bound in England by CPI Group (UK) Ltd, Croydon, CR0 4YY

CONTENTS

Recent Books by the Author include

Watching Brief (2010)
Recollections of a Sportswriter (2009)
The History of Australian Cricket (2008)
Rugby Clubs and Grounds (2005)
English Rugby Clubs (2004)
Britain's Rugby Grounds (2003)
Australian Cricket History (2003)
Reminiscences of a Sportswriter (2002)
Menston Actually (2001)
Sports Books in Britain (2000)
Ramblings of a Sportswriter (1999)
A Year in the Sporting Pressbox (1998)
The Twickenham Papers (1997)
A Sportswriter's Year (1997)
Sporting Heritage (1996)
One Day in Leicester (1995)
A History of Australian Cricket (1993)
Cricket Indulgence (1991)
History of South Australian Cricket (1990)
South African International Cricket (1989)
Two Tours and Pollock (1988)
Seven Tests (1987)
Australians in South Africa (1987)
Cricket Safari (1986)
Australian Cricket Journal (1985)
Cricket Rebels (1985)
The History of the Sheffield Shield (1984)
The Fight for the Ashes (1983)
Cathedral End (1979)

In Preparation

A History of Baily's Magazine of Sports and Pastimes
(due for publication in mid-2014)

INTRODUCTION

It is now forty-six years since my first title appeared in print and in that time I dread to think about the number of words which have come from my various typewriters and keyboards. The upshot is that this is my fifty-sixth book and it most certainly will not be the last. I have quite a number of future works in mind so long as my publishers stop putting new ideas into my head or keep asking for books which are not on my schedule.

I did not move into writing seriously about sport until the late-1970s. I had had a few articles about cricket published in magazines such as *The Bulletin*, *Cosmopolitan* (when it was a serious production), *National Times* and even the *Journal of the Royal Commonwealth Society*. But it was the offer of the editorship of a cricket magazine which moved me away from writing about social and economic history and into sport on a full-time basis.

Cricket provided me with a completely new perspective on not just the game but the people involved with it: its spectators, its administrators, its media, its camaraderie, its hierarchy, its societies, its clubs, its players, its groupies, its shysters, and, alas, its corruption.

My fifteen years involved solely with the game provided me with the opportunity to see the world. I toured all over the place and left remaining friendships in countries as far away as Australia, New Zealand, South Africa, Hong Kong, Canada and (poor) Zimbabwe.

During these years I also worked in radio for organisations ranging from the *South African Broadcasting Corporation*, the *Australian Broadcasting Corporation*, the *Macquarie Broadcasting Network* and even dear old *BBC Radio Four*. For eleven years I had my own Saturday morning sports programme and in that time interviewed a who's who of sporting personalities.

Then, in the early 1990s, I moved into rugby league, football and rugby union and made many new friends and contacts working in those areas. I started a sports agency in London and after two years amalgamated with a Lancashire based agency to become *National Sports Reporting*.

For most of that decade I was working within the top echelons of all of my four sports and although enjoying it immensely, found that after a while it all became much of a muchness. I also realised that some sports did not have a decent trade newspaper so, along with others, we took the plunge in 1999 and founded *Rugby Times*, a weekly rugby union publication.

Although I had reported on a number of English non-league football matches over the years it was not until I wound down my coverage of Premiership and Football League fixtures did I take more to the game at its grass-roots level. Now I am addicted to it and nowadays it would not cross my mind to go to any of the super-stadia which have been created for the top level teams.

As I attempt to wind down to working only six days a week I can reflect on those great games I have witnessed in the past. In cricket it would have to be the Australia versus England Test match played in Melbourne in December 1982 which the visitors won by three runs: In rugby league the 2002 Grand Final at Old Trafford when Bradford lost to St.Helens in the last seconds of the match due to an awful error by the referee: In rugby union it is a dead-heat between the great Test match between New Zealand and the British Lions at Lancaster Park, Christchurch in 1983 and the Currie Cup clash between Western Province and Northern Transvaal at Newlands, Cape Town in 1985.

However, it is football which is my greatest love. The epic Wembley final of 1998 between Charlton Athletic and Sunderland will forever be in my memory for the eight goals scored and then such a remarkable and dramatic penalty shoot-out. But topping all of these is a match between two non-league sides: Stamco (now defunct) and Tiverton Town in an FA Vase tie played in Hastings on a damp Sunday in mid-January 1995.

It was a clash which had everything. Emotion, an early red card, tension, a record crowd, seven goals, a chairman with tears rolling down his cheeks, the holders of the Vase defeated, an incredibly vocal crowd. Even now, years later, the game is still talked about in non-league circles.

My wife and I moved to Carmarthen three years ago and although I had visited the Richmond Park ground a number of times in a professional capacity I thought I could now just sit and watch matches. How wrong I was, for within a very short time I started getting involved with the club and now hold the post of Director of Communications.

This book is a personal chronicle of a twelve month period in the life of a Welsh Premier League club. It has been a fascinating time and very much a learning curve for someone who usually just sits in pressboxes.

However, my Multi-Media Centre situated at the back of the main stand has now become a meeting place at every half-time break where friends and acquaintances have little problem in sampling my wife's home-made cakes.

Do come and join us.

Braemar House
Carmarthen   July 2013

6

JACK HARDING
(1894-1976)

John Myles Harding was born in 1894 in the coal mining village of Trimdon in County Durham. At two years of age his mother passed him over to the Harding family who raised him until he was old enough to start work in the nearby Trimdon Grange Colliery.
Jack, as he was always known, worked in the mines for seven years until he enlisted in the army at the beginning of the First World War. A keen sportsman, he played for Trimdon Colliery Football Club and made many appearances in Wearside League matches. The colours of the Trimdon side were black and gold which, in later years, Jack would designate as the colours of Carmarthen Town.

As soon as he completed his basic training Jack was posted to Carmarthen and was based in the army barracks by the side of the River Towy in Johnstown. During this time he met Mary Elizabeth John (who was known as 'May') and in 1915 they announced their engagement. However, Jack was soon called up for combat duty.

His active military career was cut short when he was captured while fighting in Belgium. Taken to a prisoner-of-war camp in Germany he was detained for over two years before being released in 1917 and repatriated to England. In this period Jack was listed as 'Missing Presumed Dead,' and it was only news of his release which stopped May from marrying somebody else.

Shortly after his return the now Sergeant Harding of the Welsh Guards became batman to Sir Grismond Philipps who, in later years, became Lord Lieutenant of Carmarthenshire. This arrangement lasted until Jack left the army eighteen months later and during this time he had lodgings in Priory Street.

After their marriage Jack and May lived initially in Quay Street before moving to Lime Grove. Jack worked for the General Post Office for the rest of his career and on retirement he purchased a bakery round. When this got too much he found employment on the town's weighbridge.

In the Second World War both he and May were in uniform. Jack, by now, was Company Sergeant Major in charge of the Carmarthen Army Cadets with May running the female Auxiliary Territorial Service. The cadets were based in a Nissen hut in Penllwyn Park.

When Jack joined the GPO in 1919 there were a number of football teams based in Carmarthen. At one time there were four clubs with the name St.Peters in their title, all of whom played on land where the car park is today. However, it was always said that if you played football you worked for the GPO: if you played rugby your job was with the GPO Engineers.

During the 1920s the two major teams were St.Peters and Quay Rovers and in 1930 they decided to amalgamate to become St.Peters Rovers. This was a Carmarthen side in all but name with Jack Harding being at the forefront of every move. The club folded with the onset of war.

Soon after the war was over an attempt was made to form a Carmarthen Athletic club. Although they gained membership of the Carmarthenshire League the club soon fell into abeyance.

It was Jack Harding who had the enthusiasm to found the Carmarthen Town club as we know it today. In 1950 he appointed the talented Stan Goldsmith as captain and recruited other well known local names such as the Wentmore and Turner brothers. He arranged for games to be played Penllwyn Park for two seasons until Richmond Park was created in 1952.

Our home ground was at that time divided by a large hedge which ran from (what is now) goal to goal. On one side was the New King George Field and on the other was waste land where the curator of the Old Quay Street Museum used to spend his days looking for Roman Pottery. For the first few seasons Jack made sure that bandages were available when games were taking place as players would find their legs cut on shards of the protruding pottery.

In 1953 the club joined the Welsh League and Jack appointed Len Emanuel as manager. The committee used to meet in the Bunch of Grapes and consisted of Albert Davies, Jimmy Hughes, Bob Parry, Aneurin Parry, Bill Wright and Jack as chairman. Their aim was to give the public good football and they were rewarded with regular crowds in excess of 3,000 spectators. During the 1950s, with only one team being promoted, Carmarthen had the frustration of finishing runners-up for six successive seasons.

As the club developed Jack started taking more of a back seat role although he was still to be found on the terraces at matches well into old age. He died in 1976 in the old Priory Street Hospital. May died in 1982.

Jack is buried in the old part of Carmarthen Cemetery. His grave has no headstone but has a flat stone border marking out his resting place.

Without Jack's vision and enthusiasm who knows what may have been in its place. He is our founder and, for that, we must all give thanks.

FORGETTABLE MEMORIES

Well, thank goodness that's over with. What a season 2011/12 turned out to be for the Old Gold. The first half was awful beyond belief while the second part became better as the weeks rolled on.

When you are sitting in pressboxes around the country the game panning out in front of you seems nothing like it does to the supporters who wait anxiously for the outcome. From the stand a referees' assessor analyses the match in a certain way; journalists from a totally different viewpoint; while the punters from each club only see what they want to see.

The referee is always wrong, say those from the terraces. Respective managers cannot understand why decisions are given against them while the poor fourth official is there to get ninety minutes of ear-bashing in between holding up his electronic board. As an Aberystwyth Town fan eloquently shouted out: "Whose side are you on, ref?"

It was the last pre-season friendly, against Bryntirion Athletic, which had first caused me to raise my eyebrows. A solitary goal two minutes from time against a club from the Welsh League was lucky enough but the fact was that they had played us off the park. By the fourth league match, a 6-1 defeat on the North Wales coast against Prestatyn Town, I knew that there had to be changes.

My notebook records an incident from that game which took place just before half-time with the home team leading 4-0. I remember looking up from the pressbox and gazing across the pitch to the away dugout. Our then manager, instead of following the events unfolding in front of him, was sitting bowed down with his head in his hands. I've been reporting for over forty years and I know when I see a defeatist attitude.

Back in Carmarthen I mentioned what I had seen and over the following weeks let the powers-that-be know that they were slowly but surely losing the support of the terraces. Gates were declining and only the faithful were going to away matches to see yet another defeat.

Something had to be done. Word came (albeit unofficially) from the Football Association of Wales (FAW) and the Welsh Premier League (WPL) that a club like Carmarthen Town would be a huge loss if relegated. Not only that but South West Wales needed a club like ours playing top grade football. Whatever those at Haverfordwest County thought of these whispers I dare not consider.

It got to the stage in late-November when I felt that I should say something. After a 5-2 home defeat to Afan Lido I stormed my way around the pitch and thumped my way up the stairs and into the clubhouse bar. Fortunately for the club's president he was busy entertaining important sponsors otherwise the poor man would have received my verbal opinions.

Behind the scenes things had been happening. I had got wind of a meeting with a potential new manager and coach but that had come to nothing. Then the name of a former player, Neil Smothers, cropped up. "He could be a coach," I was told. Two days later I was sitting in the clubhouse at Port Talbot Town when I first heard Mark Aizlewood mentioned. He had been connected with the club in the past and appeared willing to take over and to sort out the mess.

The timing of the change, when it came, surprised quite a few people as we had just claimed a rare win, albeit in the Welsh Cup over Bridgend Town of the Welsh League. After the Friday evening match the guillotine crashed down: Neil Smothers was officially appointed first-team coach the next day.

Neil was returning to the club he had left eighteen months earlier in order to travel around Australia. Born in Newport in 1977, he had played in the Welsh Premier League for Inter Cardiff, Cwmbran Town and Port Talbot Town before moving to Richmond Park in 2004. Neil had played in 215 matches in both midfield and defence scoring six goals in the process.

His first match in charge was away to Airbus Broughton, a club whose ground is situated just to the west of Chester. What he must have thought as Carmarthen scored after just forty-one seconds would be guesswork but by the time a 3-1 defeat had sunk in he no doubt knew the task ahead of him.

Mark Aizlewood was appointed at the end of the first week in January 2012. He became the seventh manager of Carmarthen Town since they had entered the top flight of Welsh football in 1996. His predecessors had been Wyndham Evans, John Mahoney, Tomi Morgan (twice), Andrew York, Mark Jones and Deryn Brace.

It was not the first time that Aizlewood had been part of the Carmarthen coaching staff. He first joined in 2003 as assistant to Andrew York before leaving to become assistant manager to Ian Rush at Chester City. He returned to be assistant to Deryn Brace and was also appointed as the club's academy director before departing again in late 2009 to pursue his business interests.

Mark was born in Newport in 1959 and made his debut as a central defender for Newport County in 1975. He then travelled around the football circuit plying his trade at Luton Town, Charlton Athletic, Leeds United, Bradford City,

Bristol City, Cardiff City, Merthyr Tydfil, Aberystwyth Town, Newport AFC and Cwmbran Town. In twenty-six years he scored twenty-five goals.

He won thirty-nine caps for Wales during his nine year international career playing in both World Cup and European Championship qualifying matches. Before that he had twice represented Wales in Under-21 fixtures.

Like so many former footballers Mark has had some well publicised ups-and-downs in both his playing career and private life. Whatever has happened in the past is totally irrelevant to the position he has now taken up at Richmond Park. He has attracted comment from numerous sources most of which have been favourable. His ability as a media analyst is highly regarded but there is a quote on a Newport County message-board which is worth repeating. It says: 'Mark Aizlewood is the best football coach in South Wales by a million miles.'

At the moment Gareth Owen Jones (G.O.) is both the Carmarthen Town chairman and secretary. In a statement issued on the appointment Gareth said: "We welcome Mark back to Richmond Park. He knows we face a big battle ahead to avoid relegation but our executive committee are sure that he is up to the task."

Mark's first league match in the dug-out was the late-January clash at Aberystwyth. The Welsh Premier League had split in half and we were in the relegation section. New signings had come into the club and the difference was starting to show. The Old Gold went two goals up only to be pegged back to a 2-2 draw. This mattered little to me as I could now proudly send out texts proclaiming: "I have seen Carmarthen get an away point."

Right up until the beginning of March I was filing stories to my sports agency proclaiming that: "Carmarthen are still unbeaten in the league in 2012." Then came a horrible defeat at the seaside when Afan Lido stuffed us 5-1 on a cold Friday night. Two wins and two defeats followed until a visit to Chester in early April.

Jeff Thomas and Gareth Jones

It was Easter Saturday and everything had gone right for me earlier in the day. Not only had I visited a country bookshop in the heart of Cheshire and purchased some very rare titles but I had also found an old English delicacy in a quaint bakery and so enjoyed a perfect lunch.

It is days such as this in which you know, just know, that everything is going to be all right. We were playing Airbus yet again and there seemed to be an air of invincibility about us. Airbus were muted and after an hour's play Carmarthen scored. For the next half an hour the roll of the dice went the way of the visitors. As the referee blew his final whistle I sent out the news to my fellow agency reporters: 'I have seen Carmarthen win away.' Some of the replies I received straight back were lacking my enthusiasm.

Two further successive wins, another of which was away, saw Carmarthen finish the season in eleventh position but only on goal difference. What Mark and Neil had done was little short of brilliant in the circumstances.

Of all the new signings the one which raised the most eyebrows was that of thirty-eight year old Julian Alsop. A much travelled journeyman footballer, who had played for fourteen different clubs since 1990, he was brought out of retirement to bring a different type of character into the dressing room.

The best description I have found about Julian came from Martin Allen, his former manager at Cheltenham Town. In an interview with the *Gloucestershire Echo* in 2009, Allen gave his reason for signing Alsop for the club. "We went shopping for a big strong centre-forward at the start of the season, but couldn't afford the players we wanted. If you go shopping in a supermarket and ask for a fillet steak, but can't afford it, you have to find something else and we've ended up with a gristly old fatty lump of lard up front: but it tasted good."

Neil Smothers

However, the season might have been over on the pitch but there were still twists and turns to come. News had come through that a number of applicants for a UEFA and WPL licence had failed at the first time of asking. They were going to appeal to an independent panel. Should one of the current WPL clubs fail to meet the criteria then we were saved from relegation.

Another twist concerned the Welsh League. Haverfordwest County had gained the necessary licence qualification and should they finish in one of the top two promotion spots then we would be the one to suffer. It got tense as they went on an unbeaten run.

There were a significant number of Carmarthen Town officials and supporters watching Haverfordwest's final league game away at Bryntirion Athletic. Before the match Mark Aizlewood had given an interview which appeared on the WPL website. "I feel that it would be an absolute tragedy if we were now to go down," he said. "I could not have asked for more from everybody concerned with the club both on and off the field of play. We have played ten league games, won six, drawn one and lost three which has yielded nineteen points."

He continued: "The results and facts speak for themselves since the arrival of the new management team as they do before our appointment, in which there were three wins from twenty games played and not one single point away from home; which is poor to say the least."

Haverfordwest won the game by a single goal and afterwards we watched as Mark gave a typically blunt interview to the *Sgorio* camera crew who had been filming the match. We all knew that our fate on the field was now in the hands of Taff's Well who had to gain four points from their remaining two fixtures to finish in second place in the league.

Three days later I was sitting in my office staring at a blank computer screen. I needed inspiration in order to start writing an essay on early Victorian literature when the mobile 'phone burped out its sound of a cat being strangled. It was a text from G.O. 'Carmarthen are in the WPL next season,' he wrote. 'Keep it confidential until the announcement is made on the WPL website.'

Then I realised. It was the day of the licence appeals. It did not take me too long to find out that, not surprisingly, Neath had lost out. Their finances had been dodgy all season with some well publicised dealings with Her Majesty's Revenue & Customs (HMRC). We were saved.

Mark soon had some thoughts posted on the WPL website. He commented as to how delighted he was to escape relegation but also how his joy was tinged with regret for the fate of the full-time players at Neath. "Football has a habit of giving you great highs and terrible lows in your career," he said. "I have played in World Cup matches for my country; FA Cup semi-finals; play-off finals for the Premiership and won championships, but I can honestly say that when I got the text from my chairman it was the best feeling of all and I am not too proud to admit I shed a tear."

*Mark
Aizlewood*

"I am a believer in fate and believe that because the people who run Carmarthen Town are honourable (and they have never missed a player payment; very rare these days in the league) that sometimes you get in life what you deserve and the people and players of the club did not deserve to go down."

Mark also revealed that the day following the Bryntirion match, which could have relegated his club, he attended a pre-arranged budget meeting at Richmond Park with the Carmarthen hierarchy. "A Welsh League-level budget was never on the agenda. The budget was agreed for the 2012/13 season at the same level as the previous management started with for 2011/12. Many clubs would have been looking to cut the budget not sustain it at the same level having nearly had their fingers burned."

"There is a big rebuilding job to do and we are already talking to existing and new players to ensure that the club never finds itself in this position again."

The twists to the season went on for a few more days. Taff's Well drew their penultimate game with their final fixture due to be played three days later. Now it was Newtown's turn to sweat as they had finished twelfth and last in the WPL. A Taff's Well win and there would be no relegation. The Tuesday came, and so did a thunderstorm which caused the match to be postponed. Forty-eight hours later I was sitting in the clubhouse with G.O. watching a Youth Team game when our webmaster, Huw Davies, sent a text with the news that Taff's had won 5-1.

So, after all the anxiety and nail-chewing, the two bottom placed clubs had been reprieved. The only change in the WPL for 2012/13 would be Connah's Quay replacing Neath.

What had all the fuss been about?

Huw Davies

SUMMER

It was the first Monday in May when I noticed that my email in-box told me I had an unopened message from Mark Aizlewood. I had seen him the previous Friday evening at the club's Presentation Evening and had no recollection of discussing anything which needed immediate attention.

I opened it up and there before me was a detailed assessment of his ideas for post-season fitness and relaxation. A pre-season schedule then followed. I felt tired just reading it. The first get-together was scheduled for 20 June with various training days thereafter. Various pre-season games were pencilled in during a four week period starting in mid-July followed by the opening league match on 18 August.

Then came the details of how to relax properly followed by instructions on starting to get fit again. 'Reduce calorie intake' was an interesting point and then Mark had written as to how to slowly build up strength. It was instructive for me as this would be the first time I had ever been with a group of footballers during such a period.

Football politics has never really been a part of my life. Along with others I have laughed at the self-important old boys strutting around in their blazers; on the breast pockets of which would be sewn a large badge signifying which association or league they represented. At any match they would always be first into the boardroom at half-time for their free food and after the game would enjoy further complimentary hospitality.

But away from them there are thousands who devote a large part of their lives to the administration and betterment of the game. These are the unsung heroes and without them there would be none of the organised football which most people take for granted.

This had been recognised by the National Assembly for Wales through the Communities, Equality and Local Government Committee (CELGC). This committee set up an inquiry into the Welsh Premier League and before it held any sessions had asked for submissions from interested parties. Most were rather tedious to read but two of them are worth mentioning: those from the FAW and our own (then) chairman.

The FAW paper contained some interesting points but was basically an exercise in both praising themselves and begging for more money. At no point did they mention that if any Association, League or Club did anything of which they did not approve then a 'Golden Vote' could be applied to veto such moves. I was always under the impression that the FAW had been formed to do the bidding of others, not the other way around. Ah, well.

The FAW argued that the WPL had been reduced to twelve clubs "in order to improve playing standards and competition." They pointed out that since the advent of the WPL the infrastructure of clubs had improved as had the facilities at grounds. The television deal with *S4/C* was praised although no mention was made of the cost and inconvenience to clubs whose matches were televised, and there was certainly no addressing the fact that the original television contract omitted to record the need for a facility fee to the clubs.

The latter part of the FAW paper warbled on about their push to move the WPL season to the summer months; the complete lack of media interest (other than *S4/C*); and the amount of money paid out to clubs to support their Academies which averaged out to £18,688 in 2011 with less due for forthcoming seasons.

By the time I had finished reading what was, in reality, a propaganda exercise my eyelids were drooping with boredom. In my years of living in England many bulky Football Association reports had been a wonderful source for lighting my garden incinerator. I was of the feeling this could soon add to the pile.

I turned to Gareth's paper hoping it would be better. It was: it was much better. It took him little time to address the views of the most important people in the game after the players: he wrote about the supporters and their feelings. Without these people hardly any club would survive.

Gareth stated: "As a club, Carmarthen had doubts about cutting the WPL to twelve teams. We abstained from voting at the key meeting, but given that the FAW had the casting vote, we knew what the outcome would be. After two seasons, the feeling among our fans (based on detailed research) was that more teams were needed. They find watching the same clubs four times a season to be boring. The general view is that sixteen is the ideal number along with a high-quality League Cup."

This was good stuff. I was enjoying it: I like a bit of rebellion. Gareth carried on to reject "the notion of summer football" while calling for "more midweek games" and using bank holiday weekends to the full. He criticised the fact that "players can no longer sign up to play for two clubs," explaining that in the past Carmarthen liked to maintain a large squad and could "collaborate with other clubs to keep players fit and to develop young players who were too old for youth teams."

I was wide awake now as I read on. "Personally," said Gareth, "I feel that there is insufficient support for the WPL within the corridors of the FAW. We feel frustrated when decisions are made without consultation such as who is allowed to play in the Welsh Cup."

Well, that's his chances of making it into the boardrooms of power dashed for the foreseeable future. It didn't finish there as he went on to criticise the lack of WPL coverage in the press; the fact that the BBC never mentions the league or its clubs and made a pertinent conclusion: "This is the time to ask what role is played by the FAW Marketing Officer? No one has ever seen him in Carmarthen for him to share his skills. We must also ask why an expert had to be recruited, using grant funds from the 'Grow Your Club' project?"

I loved it, but it got even better when Gareth and Gwynfor Jones (Bangor City secretary) appeared before the Committee in Cardiff on 9 May 2012. Both really said their piece and I have little doubt that all interested parties would have noted their views. They each stated that they felt the WPL should expand; discussed the early-season forays into European competition; and the need to improve the standard of play. Gareth then went out on a limb to argue for the need to include "the football hotbed of Merthyr" into the system.

For exactly one hour Gareth was able to put his points and explain his reasoning for what he wrote in his submitted paper. Hardly anyone back in Carmarthen knew he had put in hours of work both to write his report and to travel to the Welsh Assembly building to put his club's point of view. In days past the local newspaper would have put such matters on to the news pages, let alone the sports section. They would have been proud to give publicity to such an event. Not any more: the silence from the *Carmarthen Journal* was deafening.

I was inspired, so on 24 May I went to Stebonheath Park in Llanelli to attend a CELGC meeting. This was the first of two such gatherings called by the Committee in order to allow any interested parties to give their points of view. The second was going to be held in Llandudno for people in North Wales to have their say.

Kevin Morris

The problem with such evenings is that first of all you have to allow the locals to let off steam about their parochial problems. This took exactly half of the time allocated and was quite frustrating for those present who had more objective matters to raise. When the time came for them to have their say the discussion ranged from summer football to 3G pitches; and from salary caps to the lack of media coverage (with a few honorable local exceptions).

I raised a few issues which I had observed from occupying pressboxes around Wales. The obvious one to me was the illusion being given out that the WPL was the equal of the English Football Conference. It is not. In the view of myself and others who have experienced the game from both sides, the level (and the style of play) is at least two steps lower: the equivalent of the Southern League Premier Division.

That opinion did not find full favour in the room although my comments on a twelve-team league being boring, as clubs were continually playing each other, went down very well. As all agreed: it is no wonder attendances are falling without any variety.

While all this was going on Carmarthen Town's General Manager, Kevin Morris, had been sorting out the list of retained players. Along with Mark Aizlewood and first-team coach Neil Smothers they had agreed to offer terms to Julian Alsop, Jack Christopher, Iestyn Evans, Paul Fowler, Tim Hicks, Jonathan Hood, Nicky Palmer, Corey Thomas and Sam Wilson.

Then there were the six new signings. I must admit to have been thrown by at least two of them as, in my journalistic capacity, I report widely on Welsh football and cannot remember having seen anyone scouting for the club at most of the matches I attended. I wonder who it is?

The first of the six was Steve Cann from Aberystwyth Town. The twenty-four year old South African goalkeeper had started his career with Derby County and had also played for Rotherham United. Also signed was thirty-one year old Leon Jeanne whose twelve previous clubs included Cardiff City, Newport County and Bath City. Leon was one of four players signed from Afan Lido the others being Carl Evans, Anthony Finselbach and Craig Hanford. The final addition to the squad was Danny Thomas from Bridgend Town.

It was only a few months ago I had been to report on a match at Aberystwyth Rugby Club and had been treated with complete contempt. Some three hours later, and less than half a mile away, at the football club I had found cheerful and friendly faces and a welcome which was genuine.

I was in the town again on Saturday 9 June, at the Marine Hotel, for the Annual General Meeting of the Welsh Premier League. There were many familiar acquaintances in the room and quite a few more whose faces I could now put to names. The League's retiring Secretary, John Deakin, handed me copies of various reports which I then read with interest.

It was a fairly standard resume of the year until I got to the following paragraph: 'One concern which has been prevalent during the past season has been the payment of players, with numerous approaches being made to the FAW by contracted players who complained that clubs had not adhered to their contractual obligations. This is a situation which cannot be allowed to continue and makes the planned enhanced management of clubs' finances by the FAW totally justifiable.'

Not paying players is something which seems to dominate late-season gossip so this came as no surprise. However, what John wrote next was dynamite. He said: 'I have also again had to write to clubs regarding suspicions of illegal betting and this is being closely monitored in liaison with the Gambling Commission. Any individual found to be involved will undoubtedly face serious sanctions from the governing body.'

Well, that was a beauty. I only knew of one match in the past season which had been thrown for betting purposes and the players involved won so little money it really had not been worth the trouble. I asked John if he could give me any hints on the other games but he just smiled and changed the subject.

When this report was tabled at the meeting not one club delegate spoke on the matter, while two representatives seemed to suddenly be most interested in the ornate ceiling.

The meeting was also told that a new television deal had been agreed and for the next three years, at least, clubs would get a facility fee of £1000 each time they hosted the *S4/C* cameras. In Carmarthen terminology this would be the equivalent of an extra two hundred people paying at the gate.

When it came to discussing the size of the WPL the hierarchy pushed the barrel hard for a continuation of twelve clubs. We were given examples of a

John Collyer

number of Eastern European leagues who had the same number of teams. There was dissatisfaction from delegates and in the time-honoured way of kicking a problem into the long grass the WPL announced that there would be a paper prepared by the FAW's Head of Competitions Andrew Howard. The beauty of this revelation was the announcement that "it would not be available until late next season." Why? was my thought. It could be done in a month.

Gareth Jones stated quite clearly that Carmarthen supporters were most unhappy with the current state of affairs and said: "We are worried that the clubs will not be consulted before decisions are made." Club President Jeff

17

Thomas also expressed his concerns: "Eleven of the twelve clubs within the league have seen a drop in their attendances since the new structure was introduced. Our fans do not want to see the same teams several times a season and are voting with their feet."

What struck me as very rude was that the views of both Carmarthen delegates were seemingly ignored and a point was raised from the head table which said: "The financial pot is currently divided by twelve. Do you really want it divided by sixteen?" So: It all boils down to greed, does it?

When I got back to my office I had a check on the attendances of the Eastern European Leagues which comprised twelve clubs or less. In all cases, especially in Estonia, familiarity was breeding contempt.

The following Tuesday evening it was our turn to hold an Annual General Meeting. Gareth put forward new proposals for the structure of the club which received unanimous approval. "As I mentioned in the public meetings, the club had become stagnant and needed to be invigorated. Hopefully with the support of some new faces and continued support from the current volunteers, we can ensure that the club strives once more to get to the upper echelons of the league and gain a European place."

Then Mark Aizlewood took over. He outlined the challenges facing the team on the field during the coming months. He mentioned that all members of last season's squad had been invited to pre-season training and hinted that three other signings were imminent.

A few days later we found out their names. All were from the now defunct Neath club and the three could not be signed until the liquidator and FAW had agreed upon their contractual release. They were Matthew Rees, Ian Hillier and Craig Hughes. This brought the first-team squad to eighteen when you add the nine still with the club from last season.

Quite a number of people turned up to watch the first pre-season training session. There were around twenty players present and a number of the backroom team. Mark started barking out instructions fairly quickly and after a while it became clear that a few of the younger members of the squad were finding the going tough. The two hour session ended with a scratch match being played in pouring rain which resulted in the Lime Green Jacket side defeating the Red Jackets 4-2.

Away from the training ground Mark had also been utilising the internet. On the WPL website he had spoken about his thoughts for the forthcoming season and gazed into his crystal ball. There was some trepidation in his views when he said: "Any team which finishes above TNS, Bangor City and Llanelli will qualify for Europe. That is certain. The top three will consist of these teams."

Turning to Carmarthen Town he used reverse psychology to make his point: "Last season we scored the fewest number of goals in the league; had the least draws; conceded over sixty goals and had the most defeats of anybody. However, while we have not got the signature signings, or the big sponsor to fund them, we remain ambitious and believe that the squad we have assembled will hopefully ensure that we are not in a relegation battle next year."

"We will have to rely on organisation, discipline, team-spirit, character and all of the other attributes you can instill into a squad of players. Only time will tell as to how far up the league they can take you."

Training nights then moved into 'the Barn,' a massive enclosed building owned by Carmarthen Athletic Rugby Club. The floor inside is covered by 'Third Generation'(3G) turf which means it is perfect for the players to both train and to play scratch matches. For those who came to watch, the evenings always proved to be a pleasant time as well as being wonderful gossip sessions.

Jonathan Lewis

The first two pre-season matches were arranged for Saturday 14 July, against Barry Town and West End, with staggered kick-off times. The morning game was played on a fenced 3G pitch at Aberthin Road in Cowbridge which gave me an opportunity, prior to kick-off, to walk around the town. I had not visited before but had heard that it was rather an up-market part of the Vale of Glamorgan.

After finding numerous coffee shops and tapas bars, as well as restaurants whose menu prices made me laugh, I sent a text to the office stating: 'This really is Chelsea-on-Taff' and that was even before I had made the acquaintance of Henry.

He must have been about seven years old and was having quite a tantrum when I stopped to watch him. He was with his parents who were talking to another couple. While Henry was having his convulsions they were chatting about a local art show which was about to take place. I ignored all of the pretentious twaddle because I found myself captivated by the clothes, and hat, which Henry was wearing. I happened to know that the hat cost around £200 and I guessed that his designer clothes gave very little change from a four figure sum. Poor Henry: life is so tough.

Cowbridge Comprehensive School was not as large as I expected it to be but at least it had sufficient grounds for a number of sports. After getting the names of the players in both teams I was able to join the other three Carmarthen stalwarts who had come to watch the clash with Barry Town. There was John Collyer (who writes the match reports for the *Carmarthen Journal*); Lyn Evans (who owns a cafe in Tanygroes, near Aberporth where the roast meals are highly recommended) father of Iestyn, and Alan Dodd who I seem to meet at grounds all over South Wales.

It took the Old Gold just twenty-six minutes to open the scoring when Paul Fowler put in a superb effort from thirty yards. Barry equalised five minutes later and then Fowler scored his second right on the interval. Craig Hughes added a third ten minutes after the break with Barry replying three minutes later.

Although I must confess at not being an expert on tactics or coaching there are little things which are noticeable to the untrained eye. The one which made an impression on me during the game was that Neil Smothers, playing as a central defender, seemed to be mentally sharper than most of his team. His distribution was good but quite often his team-mates did not appear to grasp quickly enough as to where the ball was going. Maybe things will improve.

At the final whistle it was off to Llandarcy for the second fixture. The rain, which had been fairly light, now hammered down but made not the slightest difference to the spacious 3G pitch on which the game against West End was going to be played.

The Llandarcy Academy of Sport is situated in a fine modern building which consists of a multi-use sports hall and equipment for numerous other activities. The whole development cost £6,000,000 to construct and was financed by a number of funding bodies. It seems incredible to reflect that in 1940 this whole area had been razed to the ground by the German Luftwaffe.

The number of Carmarthen supporters had risen to around fifty by the time the match started and it took only eight minutes for Liam Thomas (another new signing) to give the Old Gold the lead. He added a second ten minutes later and just before the break West End pulled a goal back with a well taken penalty kick.

While the teams were sitting around during the interval I spotted a West End player whose face seemed familiar. It took a while to remember then it came to me. It was about a year ago that I had been at Eigen Crescent in the Swansea suburb of Townhill when his club were entertaining Cambrian & Clydach. I was sitting at the back of the stand taking my usual notes of the game when a woman, of late middle-age, had sat down on the seat in front of me. Not long afterwards she was joined by a younger woman and they started to pass the time of day.

A little later West End made a substitution and on to the field came the player whose face I had recognised. Immediately the younger of the pair turned to her companion and said: "See that lad over there? Ooh, he's so lovely. Do you know that he was only the second man ever to have my daughter?"

Sometimes, just sometimes, there are moments in your life which are so surreal that relating the incident would probably be met with scepticism and disbelief. So I kept the story to myself and walked around the Llandarcy pitch to find some shelter for the second-half.

It did not take long for Matthew Rees to head a third goal and twenty minutes later Liam Thomas completed his hat-trick. West End pulled one back near to the final whistle but the 4-2 scoreline reflected the conclusion of a good afternoon's workout.

However, it did set me wondering as to how Mark and Neil were going to judge who to keep on for the season and who to let go. I would not have a clue after watching today's two matches so it's best I write about the team and let the experts make the on-field decisions.

After training the following Wednesday Mark told three of the trialists that he would not be offering them any terms and they were free to seek another club. I was not surprised as it had been fairly clear that none were quite at WPL level. With the decision to put at least one of the three chosen Academy players on the substitutes bench, for home matches only, the first-team squad was starting to take some sort of shape.

Then came the first home pre-season friendly. Newport County were the visitors and the team they brought to Richmond Park included a number who had turned out for them at Wembley two months earlier in the FA Trophy final.

The kick-off for the match was delayed owing to traffic problems on the M4 motorway which gave me a chance to wander around the ground and chat to various people. Then, to my dread, a familiar face appeared and I knew right away that my day was going to be continually interrupted. He was on leave from his position as Third Secretary at the British Embassy in Ethiopia and was staying locally with his family. He proudly told me that he had visited every league ground in Addis Ababa and for most of the match, while I was trying to concentrate on my work, he related in minute detail the facilities at each of these venues.

After the game the general feeling among the cognoscenti was that this had been the best Carmarthen Town performance for quite a long time. The sunshine had helped following weeks of unseasonal rain and groundsman Jonathan Lewis had prepared a pitch covered with lush grass. With building work about to start on the new changing-room block, and coats of paint on walls and gates, the feeling of a bright new season was high on the agenda.

The game had started well with Jonathan Hood and Leon Jeanne putting the Old Gold two goals to the good at the interval. A penalty from Craig Hughes increased the score and although Newport pulled back a late goal the 3-1 win was a fillip for both players and supporters.

The following week Swansea City sent a team to Richmond Park. It was through the good offices of former Carmarthen goalkeeper Tony Pennock, now employed at the Swans Youth Academy, that such a strong side took to the field. The fact that all of the visiting players were full-time showed from the start and it was no surprise when they took a seventh minute lead with a superbly worked goal. However, the Old Gold came back to equalise twenty minutes later through Jonathan Hood and although each side went on to miss a number of chances the draw was a fair result.

The first weekend in August is always in my memory as the time of year for glorious sunshine; warm winds from the south-west and holidays spent watching cricket. Nowadays it seems to rain continually; the winds howl and it is the middle of pre-season football fixtures.

Taff's Well Football Club is situated in Glanyllyn and sits astride the busy main road taking traffic from Cardiff to Pontypridd. I arrived at the ground only a few minutes behind Mark Aizlewood after which the team selected for the match started to appear. It was a big day for the locals as their new stand was to have its official opening ceremony before the game started. Everything seemed well with the new structure until the rain arrived and it was then that it became obvious the levels of the concrete walkways were anything but smooth. Splashing around in a raised, covered stand was a new experience for some of us.

The team which Mark and Neil had chosen could be classified as a squad side with quite a few of the expected first-team given the day off. However, that did not get away from the fact that the Carmarthen side played some good football even when facing a nine-man defence. I was impressed by the usual suspects but what I did like was the way the three Academy players Sam Wilson, Iestyn Evans and Mitch Escott-Sloan, gained in confidence as

22

time wore on. It was Sam's through ball to Liam Thomas, a minute from full-time, which resulted in the only goal of a damp afternoon.

Sir Alfred Mond was the Member of Parliament for Carmarthen from 1924-28. He was elected as a Liberal but two years later had quite a falling out with David Lloyd George over the former Prime Minister's controversial plans to nationalise agricultural land. He then joined the Conservative party who, in 1928, raised him to the peerage as Lord Melchett.

While he was the local Member he presented the Mond Cup for which, he stipulated, "... was to be played for by football teams within the Carmarthen constituency." Nowadays a number of clubs from outside of the original area are invited to compete.

This season the Cup committee decided to have four 'Pools,' each of four teams, with the top one in each going through to play in a semi-final. Carmarthen Town's Reserves, who compete in the Second Division of the Carmarthenshire League, represent the club in this competition and were drawn away for two of their three fixtures.

The first of these took place at Station Road, St.Clears on Monday 6 August. The home team, who play in the Pembrokeshire League, gave the Old Gold a good game before eventually losing 3-0. The match was held up at the start for the referee to get treatment after having been stung by a wasp and once the game got underway it took only five minutes for Jody Thomas to give the Reserves the lead. A penalty by Richard Whalley and a third from Josh Baker wrapped up a successful evening for the visitors.

The first team squad went to play Cwmbran Town the following Saturday in their final pre-season match. The run-down Cwmbran Stadium had changed little from the last time the Old Gold had walked onto the pitch. The result way back in October 2006 was a 5-4 victory in the season The Crows started their sad decline down through four divisions from their heyday in the old League of Wales.

I asked one of the home committeemen, Mike Lewis, if I could use the pressbox at the top of the stand. "No one is allowed up there now," he told me. "The Council has decreed that if we get a crowd of 2,000 and they all push to get out by using the back stairs at the final whistle then it might be possible for there to be concrete failure."

I was a bit puzzled so I asked Mike what had been the club's average attendance recently. He looked at me with sad eyes. "Our highest last season was forty-five. We have told the Council this and they are just not interested and what is worse is that we pay three times as much as those hiring nearby Spytty Park." The irony was not lost on me.

The Carmarthen players looked fit and eager for the afternoon's contest. Within three minutes Anthony Finselbach had scored with a beautiful lob. Then Jonathan Hood put one of his usual pile-drivers past the home keeper and five minutes later Tim Hicks had an easy tap-in.

Jack Christopher came on at half-time and within five minutes had scored the visitors' fourth goal. Three more followed through Craig Hughes, Corey Thomas and Liam Thomas with Cwmbran's only shot on target for the day being substitute Craig Appleby's consolation effort ten minutes from time.

A 7-1 win is a good win in anyone's books. Mark tried not to seem too pleased after the game stating: "Pre-season overall is exactly how we planned it to be with regard to match fitness and team organisation." Well we'll soon see, won't we?

| Steve Cann | Carl Evans | Craig Hanford | Ian Hillier |
| Matthew Rees | Corey Thomas | Paul Fowler | Jonathan Hood |

EARLY DAYS

Anyone arriving at Richmond Park for the first league match of the season could easily have thought: 'Nothing changes; same faces, same programme, same burgers.' In a way they would have been right. The changes at the ground would hardly have been noticed while the lush playing field, so lovingly prepared by Jonathan Lewis, looked perfect.

Behind the scenes it was a bit different. Gareth Jones was still supposed to be convalescing following an operation to remove his gallbladder with webmaster Huw Davies taking over as Matchday Secretary. Two commentators from *BBC Radio Wales* turned up unexpectedly and had to be accommodated with the rest of the Secretary's numerous jobs having to be shared around.

Before, during and after the game every one of the club's officials and volunteers has a job to do. At the main gate the Director of Finance, Anthony Parnell, resplendent in his yellow safety jacket, is in charge of making sure that all the various turnstiles are manned; the operators have a cash float and a sufficient number of programmes are available.

The Director of Community Affairs, Paul Ashley-Jones, has the Club Shop under his charge and, when I walked in, there were two huge boxes containing the new season's kit waiting to be unpacked and put out for sale. During any match Paul is always seen going around the ground selling raffle tickets, although a lot of the work he does for the club, particularly on the charity side, goes unreported.

Anthony Parnell

Senior Steward, Andrew Thomas, is always at the ground hours before anyone else. He oversees security and keeps an eye on the many people who wander in and out in the hours prior to kick-off. Today, in particular, he might well have been needed as Mark Aizlewood had been riled by comments attributed to visiting Aberystwyth Town manager, Tomi Morgan. I won't repeat the commonly known scenario but there were some people waiting for the explosion which never came.

Once Huw had printed off the teamsheets I could wander over to my multi-media centre situated at the back of the stand and take up residence for the afternoon. The schedule follows a familiar pattern: a pre-match preview for radio, with updates and score flashes as and when needed; laying out the large pro-forma sheets for recording match statistics, and getting other paperwork ready to note all necessary detail and incidents which happen during the afternoon. Fortunately, John Collyer does the match report for the *Carmarthen Journal* so that is one burden which comes my way very infrequently.

Although the afternoon was humid the sun shone for the whole ninety minutes. It had rained heavily for much of the previous three days and Jonathan was a little concerned about how heavy the pitch might be and whether the ball would roll easily. He need not have worried: it was immaculate.

Once the players emerged from the changing rooms there was a feeling among the spectators around me that the Old Gold would be able to record their first opening game success for four years. It nearly didn't go to plan as Aberystwyth's Jordan Follows missed scoring by a whisker within thirty seconds of the start.

The first-half was somewhat attritional with each side trying to wear the other down. Carmarthen forward Jack Christopher had two good chances as well as getting his usual yellow card for dissent while debutant goalkeeper Steve Cann was giving me palpitations by venturing way out of his penalty area far too many times. On one occasion, when Cann had been left behind, a brilliant saving tackle by captain Carl Evans foiled the visitors from taking the lead.

The first twenty minutes of the second-half were flat. It was as though Aberystwyth had run out of ideas and the Old Gold confused as to what was happening. Then two incidents in a minute turned the game: Christopher headed a goal over the advancing 'keeper and Carmarthen's Matthew Rees received a straight red card for swearing at an opposing player who had kicked the ball away when he was trying to take a quick free-kick.

Rees' problem was that referee Mark Whitby was standing beside him at the time and thought that the comments were directed at him. Afterwards Rees told me he had been to see the referee and explained that the comments were made to the player and not to the official. Whitby agreed to view a tape of the incident but I am not holding my breath for a positive result.

Somehow the sending off seemed to galvanise the Carmarthen team. From then on they went into full attack mode although I am sure that Mark did not give those instructions. Seven minutes from time Liam Thomas scored a second goal and the joy on the face of the spectators said enough. After last season's debacle this was just the initial tonic they needed.

As expected, referee Whitby saw fit to ensure that Rees served a two match suspension and that, along with a number of injuries, had Mark somewhat concerned about the team he would select for the next match. This was going to be our first away league fixture of the season, against Airbus Broughton, whose ground is situated on the western outskirts of Chester.

I missed training during the week as I had been away in Liverpool on publishing business. Thankfully my wife was able to deal with the twenty or so emails which hit my Inbox on a daily basis as well as liaising with Mark on the various press releases he wanted circulated. I also had to forgo seeing the Mond Cup match at Johnstown where Steve (Gas) Jones' reserve team had notched up a convincing 4-0 victory.

We all gathered outside the (now boarded up) old clubhouse building in Priory Street at what seemed like dawn on the final Saturday in August. It wasn't really dawn, that's just me exaggerating the fact I had to get up early. I don't do mornings but if I wanted to join the others on the team coach to Broughton then I had to be on time.

Andrew Thomas

As soon as I arrived I was joined by the club's previous vice chairman Alun Williams. Then came the usual suspects in Howard Williams (a former manager), Jonathan Lewis, Alan Latham (who had served the club as secretary for twenty-six years), Peter 'the fruit' Williams, David 'Dai-Bala' Hughes and Andrew Thomas. Kit-man Gareth Davies was already on board the coach when it arrived and en-route we picked up Anthony Parnell and Jeff Thomas. Brian Davies and entourage joined us at the ground.

The first stop on any away trip is Rhayader where an excellent breakfast is always ready for us at *The Strand Bistro*. Everyone, without exception, had what is called a 'the full works' although I might add that there was mirth amongst the unenlightened when I ordered cappuccino instead of the regulation tea or coffee.

Mark Aizlewood was already in-situ when we arrived along with a number of players who had driven across country to meet us. It is an unwritten rule that we leave the players alone on these trips which then gives the management team a chance to talk to any of them individually.

The people who run the Airbus Broughton club gave us their usual friendly welcome when we pulled up outside the ground. It was handshakes all round as two groups of us headed in separate directions: players, management and myself towards the changing rooms while the rest went and enjoyed the lavish hospitality of the company's social club.

The pressbox has plenty of room but is, unfortunately, virtually at ground level. That is fine until you get people sitting, then standing, in front of you. I can usually spot these folk a mile away and was correct in my assumption when, twenty minutes from the start, the day's mascot arrived.

No problem there but he was accompanied by his parents; his elder brother; grand-parents; his mother's brother and wife, and two elderly great-uncles. After the usual preliminaries prior to kick-off our little hero ran off the pitch to flashing cameras and a virtual family film crew who had recorded his every movement. They then all sat in front of the pressbox.

Being an expert on these types of situations I was able to note things on my pad. It took grandma, who had her back turned away from the game for the whole time she was with us, exactly eight minutes to ask the two young boys if they wanted a burger. On being given an order everyone stood up while she made her way along the row. Five minutes later all rose again as she returned.

One minute later, the young uncle, who had been infected by the smell, decided that he and his wife should also have a burger. More getting up as he went to join the food queue. While he was away the kids and Mum were getting restless with our mascot hero deciding to bang the unused plastic seats in a rhythmic style. Uncle returned to more bobbing up and down. As he took his seat the kids decided that they wanted to go so everyone stood up again as they departed for good. Grand-parents joined them as did the others once the burgers had been wolfed down. All that had taken just twenty-two minutes.

Fortunately most of the action on the field had been to my left, where the sightlines were good, and I had watched as Steve Cann pulled off some excellent saves. With the strong wind behind them the Airbus team were attacking well when suddenly our goalkeeper fell awkwardly and dislocated his shoulder. Cann left the field on a stretcher and Jonathan Hood was given the job between the sticks.

'Oh, Ye Of Little Faith,' goes the expression. I was concerned but at the end of the ninety minutes all I could do was to praise Hood in the highest possible manner, for his display had been as perfect as that of a qualified 'keeper. He was superb; there really is no other way to describe how he flung himself around the goal in the manner of a true professional.

Meanwhile, Corey Thomas had put the Old Gold ahead; Airbus equalised twenty minutes after the break and in the fifth minute of added time at the end of the game Liam Thomas saw his twenty-yard shot curl wickedly into the bottom left corner of the Airbus net. It was a wonderful effort which saw every team member run to congratulate him. If nothing else, the camaraderie Mark had instilled into the players then glowed like a beacon.

Realising that the team bus would be delayed, while Cann had his shoulder treated at Wrexham's Maelor Hospital, Jeff and I were able to get a lift back to Carmarthen with John Collyer. We relived the game from our own perspectives. Wow! We were top of the league.

The following Wednesday there was an Extraordinary General Meeting held at Richmond Park. Although Neil Alexander was voted in as Chairman and Gareth Jones as Director of Football there was little other business able to be conducted due to unforseen absences. No doubt another EGM will have to be arranged, when everyone is available, in order to conclude outstanding matters.

I really do like Friday night football. Years ago Tranmere Rovers used to have their 'White Nights' which were hugely popular on Merseyside. Some North Wales WPL and Cymru Alliance clubs carry on the tradition, but it is only Afan Lido in South Wales who choose to play that day on a fairly regular basis.

As it so happened, Afan Lido were our Friday visitors on the last day in August. On arriving at the ground

Steve 'Gas' Jones

many of the club's officials and helpers were already in-situ and the wheels of organisation were starting to roll. The players then appeared, having had their tactical talk from the coaching staff, and started wandering towards the changing room.

I saw Steve Cann and asked him about his shoulder as I knew it had been dislocated again while he was undergoing physiotherapy. He was not sure if he had damaged any tendons or ligaments but would know for sure early the following week. What was good to see was that most of the injured or suspended players had turned up for the match.

Once the matchday secretariat had completed their initial work and the teamsheets had been printed I did my usual perambulation around the ground to the multi-media centre. On the way I was able to have a chat with Alan Howells, who is the Afan Lido secretary in all but name; with WPL league secretary Gwyn Derfel, who was handing out the season's official handbook; and with various other familiar faces whose names keep escaping my poor memory.

Being successful, albeit for only two games, and with a high profile manager meant that the turnstiles were welcoming more spectators into the ground. We had played the same opponents four months earlier yet tonight's attendance showed an increase of 38% which was also reflected in sales of programmes and at the tea-bar.

The usual regular supporters came to sit nearby in their normal positions. I had Ifor Hughes to my left and in front were Willy Thomas, Jonathan Lewis and John Davidson. The atmosphere is always friendly and they take some of my more ridiculous comments and anecdotes with an air of tolerance.

The first half of the game was bewildering by its complete Old Gold domination. The shots rained in; the visitor's defence pulled to shreds and it was a surprise that Jack Christopher's goal had been the only score. The second period could not have been more different with Afan Lido dominating for long periods. Although Paul Fowler saw a shot rebound from the woodwork with only four minutes to go, the equaliser, when it came in injury time, was no real surprise.

Afterwards Mark Aizlewood blamed himself. "If I had done my job correctly we would have secured three points," he said. "Late in the second-half I failed as coach to make the necessary final technical adjustment which would have determined we took all three points."

There would not have been too many who might have concurred with Mark's self-assessment. As far as most were concerned seven points from three games was an excellent start to the season. However, the return match, the following Tuesday evening, would be the basis for an early evaluation of how far the team had progressed.

Still, it was not all gloom and doom as the Reserves had won 3-2 at Llandeilo with an injury time goal from Richard Whalley which added to his earlier successful penalty. Ian Bartlett was the other scorer as their season gained momentum.

Tuesday came and with it our first defeat of the season. It had been 158 pressure free days since the players had last trooped from the field with their heads down. What would have been worse for them would have been to hear the whoops of joy emanating from the home changing room. As Aize will tell you: football can be a cruel game.

The evening had started off in a manner to which I have become accustomed with plenty of stories being told as well as the usual pieces of idle chit-chat and gossip. However, from a journalistic point of view I was pleased to be told a number of things by a highly respected football administrator which completed the jigsaw-puzzle about the matches thrown last season for betting purposes. Nothing, naturally, will come from my investigations but at least I now know the name of the player who is organising the scams.

After picking up the teamsheets I went and found Gareth Jones who was standing with Neil Alexander. I completely forgot to address Neil as 'Mr Chairman' - an error which will not be repeated. Then it was up to the back of the stand to join John Collyer for the match.

Carmarthen made two changes from Friday's starting line-up with Matthew Rees back from suspension and Casey Thomas making his full debut. The Old Gold began well and then were pegged back, conceding a goal eight minutes before the break. After the resumption nothing was going right for the team which prompted Aize make three substitutions in eight minutes around the hour mark. Then, completely out of the blue, Tim Hicks scored his ninety-fifth league goal with

Howard Williams

a stubbed shot following a low cross from Jonathan Hood.

Although there were ten minutes still left on the clock neither John, nor I, were comfortable with what we were watching. A free kick deep into time added on saw Afan Lido's captain, Mark Jones, rise high above the visiting defence to head the winner past a stranded Rhys Wilson. So, twice in five days a late goal had seen us lose points, but far worse was to come.

As we muttered our way home Steve Gas's team had been down to Kidwelly to record their fourth win on the trot. Richard Whalley notched a hat-trick in a 4-0 victory, with Adam Thomas adding the icing on the cake.

Two days later Peter Fearn's Under-19 Academy team had a home pre-season friendly against Tenby. Their coach, our own Jack Christopher, was not disappointed with his youngsters' display. "There is a splendid youth set-up at Tenby," he told me later, "so a 2-0 defeat against a well drilled Carmarthen youth side was no disgrace. At Tenby there are a number of 'age' teams which attract boys from all over the community."

The alarm rang its ugly tone at sometime before six o'clock on Saturday 8 September. As I sat at the kitchen table trying hard to stay awake, and even harder not to spill my porridge, I looked at the papers on which I had listed the probable team Mark could put out on the field. It looked bad enough with five of the first-team injured and things were not going to improve as the day wore on.

We all met as usual outside the old clubhouse building in Priory Street (currently being converted into a muslim centre) and I was joined by Peter-the-fruit and Dai-Bala. When the coach eventually arrived Gareth Davies and Andrew Thomas were already on board. The only players with us were Jack Christopher and Sam Wilson.

At Rhayader we met the rest of the players and management who were already enjoying breakfast. As I happened to be somewhat 'in charge' for the day it was my job to pay the cafe's bill. What did surprise me was that most of the players had ordered orange juice and scrambled eggs. They were most restrained considering that the rest of us tucked into a full breakfast.

The journey to Prestatyn is one of the longest we have to make all season and I started to worry when the coach got caught in a lengthy queue of traffic on the main A55 at Chester. Phone calls were made telling of our possible late arrival but in the end we made it to the Bastion Gardens ground with time to spare.

The North Wales coast was bathed in sunshine. You could not have asked for a better day to play football yet things were going from bad to worse for Mark and Neil. Carl Evans had pulled out with illness first thing in the morning while Jonathan Hood had failed a fitness test. The injury crisis was getting to a critical stage.

You could sense that the Prestatyn side were aware they were not playing a full Carmarthen first-team and reacted accordingly. Their first seven shots on target were all successful with Tim Hicks' solitary reply breaking up the momentum. It was bad enough on the hour mark when Casey Thomas picked up a second yellow card. It got to the panic-button stage seven minutes later when goalkeeper Rhys Wilson was shown a straight red card for a professional foul.

As we boarded the coach for the return journey the players were quiet and restrained. Mark Aizlewood read the match statistics which clearly told him that the 7-1 defeat was nowhere near as one-sided as the score suggested. Soon we made a pit-stop where the boys stocked up with supermarket beer and food from a nearby chinese take-away. It seemed to cheer them up and at Rhayader, when most of them left us, there were apologies given out for the defeat. None of them had to do this, but they did and it was certainly a sign to me that an affinity was growing up between the new players and the supporters.

Meanwhile, back at Richmond Park the Reserves had enjoyed a 5-3 league victory over Johnstown United. Regular first-team player, Anthony Finselbach, had taken part in order to test the muscles in his back which had been causing him a problem. He scored one of the goals so at least he could be getting back towards full fitness.

The following afternoon Mark sent an email with his usual stream of consciousness for correcting and then onward distribution to all media outlets. It needed to be tidied up as always but he had some good points to make and had I been a tabloid journalist I would have made an instant headline out of "the only currently available goalkeeper we have registered is the club chef." I'm afraid to say that some time was instantly wasted in my office as my wife and I wrote out some awful

Roger Hunt

punning splashes which any decent editor would have immediately binned.

Mark, as always, spoke from the heart. "My brief for the season is to take the club forward. So even after last Saturday's game please judge me and my team at the end of the season, when I guarantee that the club will have moved forward after years of being in the doldrums."

He then mentioned the injuries: "After fantastic wins in the first two games we have suffered with injuries to key players. For instance, not once have I been able to pick the same back four. But I will work hard to rectify things. This will be considerably easier for me if our injury list clears up sooner rather than later."

Unfortunately, I had to be in Cambridge for the next three days meeting publishers so I missed watching the Under-19 Academy side defeat Cwmaman

Institute 4-3, and the Reserves win 3-1 at Penllergaer.

The middle Saturday of September arrived. Initially the day was overcast even though the sun broke through for a short while in the afternoon. Mark Aizlewood arrived at the ground early with most of the team following shortly afterwards. They went over the tactics for the day: the preparations were top class. The visitors were Llansantffraid known by their current epithet of The New Saints. The initials of TNS are misused by their opponents into such names as 'Ten Nasty Scousers,' a title we would never use in Carmarthen. The club has an impressive record having won six WPL titles in twelve years and been runners-up on four other occasions.

The match would be a challenge following the Old Gold's disastrous defeat seven days earlier. Into the team came goalkeeper Kerry Nicholas, who had been signed during the week as emergency cover; Liam McCreesh, who had returned from Australia where he had played for Northern Tigers in Sydney, and Carl Evans, back from illness.

We could hardly have asked for better media coverage for the game: as well as television, newspaper and commercial radio reporters even the BBC sent down a broadcaster who had the brief to commentate for as long as he wished.

I had set up early in the club's multi-media centre and was soon joined by Ifor and his son-in-law John Beeden. We watched the first forty-five minutes in some astonishment as Carmarthen played as though the previous week's defeat had never happened. The defence, led expertly by Carl Evans, hardly let the league champions get within sniffing distance of the goal.

It got a little tougher after the break as TNS brought on extra forwards to try and make a breakthrough. It never happened and a goalless draw was more a deserved point for us than for the visitors. Afterwards Mark said: "I knew we could get a point but towards the end I thought we might nick it with a breakaway goal."

As the first-team match was taking place so the Reserves were playing out a 2-2 draw at Abergwili, which added to their unbeaten run. On the following Monday the Under-19 side took on Llanelli at Richmond Park. It really is a wonder that any Llanelli team is surviving realising that their financial problems are going from bad to worse. Having just paid off the taxman, in order to avoid being wound up in the High Court, the club are now facing claims from all of their other creditors. My feeling is that the debt due to the Town Council for the use of Stebonheath Park is probably the most important one to meet.

As always Pam Davies looks after the turnstile, as she does for all Academy games, taking £1 from each spectator while trying to look after the match officials and running errands. As I was loitering around before the start some of these tasks were given to me.

The night was turning cold so I gave up the opportunity to stay in the open and moved upstairs into the clubhouse which meant I could sit in the warmth. With a table by one of the windows it is fairly easy to make notes although the sightlines are not perfect.

Michelle Hopkins, who is in charge of the bar, generally has an urn set on high so that coffee can be made on a whim. This let me sit peacefully for the first-half of an entertaining encounter. At the break Lyn Evans came up to discuss the match (and his son Iestyn's yellow card) and soon others had joined us. The one person I had not previously met was Martin Evans, the Welsh Schools' Football Association's Under-18 manager.

The game was a credit to the lads of both sides and would have been far better had a card-fussy referee been able to position himself better on the field. I lost count of the number of times players had to try and avoid him in order to get the ball. There were nine yellow cards sprayed around, six of which were shown to people wearing the Carmarthen colours.

As happened the previous week a goal deep into stoppage time gave the Old Gold a not quite deserved 3-2 win. However, that did not stop manager Peter Fearn from expressing his opinion about the officiating. In the changing room after the game he made a few observations: I must admit I felt he had a point.

My wife fancied a day out in Bala the following Saturday so we drove up using the coast road, arriving just before the team coach. Walking around the town it was impossible not to hear the North Wales scouse accents nor to notice that the seating areas outside most of the public houses were full to overflowing. Quite a number of the shops offered the casual tourist souvenirs of a somewhat debateable taste and value. For a town situated

Gareth Davies

within the boundaries of the Snowdonia National Park I would have expected

35

a little better. The reality was that it was all a bit tacky.

Bala Town Football Club had been promoted to the WPL in 2009, and this was Carmarthen's fourth visit to the picturesque Castle Street ground. Three goals at the first meeting had been followed by two goalless defeats so the omens were not too good.

The day did not start too well as I found myself being harangued at the entrance gate by a club official when I showed my WPL Media Pass. He let me know in no uncertain terms that I had little knowledge of my profession and when I mentioned that I had forty years experience he ranted even more. Sadly it is not that unusual to get a greeting of this kind but I certainly did not expect to receive it at Bala.

As I was writing down Aizlewood's team selection from the sheet stuck on the dressing room wall I noticed to my left the virtually hidden figure of Sam Wilson sitting in the corner. He had been a very late call-up to the squad following Jack Christopher's early morning withdrawal through illness. When I finished writing I got his attention and congratulated him on the delightful individual goal he had scored for the Youth Team the previous Monday. Poor Sam was rather embarrassed by the praise but he deserved it for his splendid display.

I walked to the secretary's office to find Ruth Crump virtually tearing at her hair for the club's computer printer was misbehaving and the printing of teamsheets was proving to be difficult. While this delay was happening she sat and answered numerous queries from people who wandered in: it was just as if I was with G.O. at a home match.

The pressbox at Bala is situated at the back of the small stand. The view is fairly good and the four of us occupying seats had plenty of desk space on which to lay out our papers. Then the game started and in front of over thirty travelling fans the Old Gold put on a woeful first-half display.

At the break Aize was furious. The changing room walls shuddered: women and children ran for their lives: grown men shook with fear: the earth quaked. "As a coach," he said later, "I very rarely criticise players, preferring instead to look at myself for the reason why the team did not perform. However, following that first-half performance, where we found ourselves three goals down after thirty-eight minutes, I read the riot act to the senior players. I felt it was them, in particular, who had let us all down."

The substitutions made for the second-half calmed things down and the match drifted along its course. Bala won 3-0, to record their first victory of the season. Ironically while all this was going on Steve 'Gas's' reserve team were knocking up a 10-1 score against Llandeilo with the prolific Richard Whalley hitting the back of the net five times.

Before the Management Committee meeting, held in the clubhouse the following Monday evening, a group of us were talking about the Academy team's match the previous day. It had been dire. Played in pouring rain against Aberdare Town the only highlight of the afternoon had been the goal scored by Mitch Escott-Sloan which put the Under-19 side through to the next round of the Welsh Youth Cup.

When I worked for a living, meetings I used to attend had set agendas and relied on participants presenting their reports in a clear and concise manner. Although this was my first Management Committee I came away thinking that I had sat through ten minutes of fact and two hours of waffle. Some reports reminded me of a tape on a continual loop, having heard the same thing at other club meetings time and again. Now I am (allegedly) retired I must learn to have more patience and to sit and smile regularly even when what I am hearing is of little interest.

Saturday rolled around once again and this time the visitors were from Bangor City. It was the penultimate day of September and we had gone from top to nearly bottom of the league in that time. I felt it was very different from last season when it had been plain to the eye that the players had little confidence in the management. Now it was different: Aizlewood, by the force of his personality, was doing his utmost to keep his injury stricken side into as cohesive a unit as possible.

Peter Williams

The Bangor players and officials had stayed locally overnight in order to save them the torturous drive down the coast road. When you are a semi-professional team this is a perfectly normal thing to do. At Carmarthen a few of the players work early on a Saturday morning so the thought of regular hotel accommodation for away fixtures is just a dream. For them it is untimely morning coach travel with late night returns.

I arrived at the ground early as, along with a photographer from the *Carmarthen Journal*, we were taking both player and action pictures during the afternoon. Soon afterwards Dave Hayes, who was broadcasting full live match commentary for *Radio Bangor*, put his head around the office door in order to get the code for his Wifi link.

The wheels of a matchday were starting to crank into motion. The players had had an early lunch and were going through training routines on the pitch. To one side goalkeeping coach Rob Thomas was making sure that Steve Cann was totally fit on his return to the team from a shoulder dislocation while the administration were ensuring that the match paperwork was completely in order.

Once I had the teamsheets it was a walk around to the multi-media centre and the usual laying out of papers and notebooks. I was fortunate today in having a very experienced producer at *Radio Carmarthenshire* who was an absolute joy to work with during the afternoon. A professional like him makes life for people like me so much easier.

Soon I was joined by the little coterie of Ifor Hughes, Willy Thomas and Jonathan Lewis amongst others and we watched in horror as Bangor took just one hundred and eight seconds to take the lead. We feared the worst but it did not come. For the next eighty-eight minutes the Carmarthen players fought and fought to try and breach the visitor's defence. It held rock solid and at the final whistle we had suffered our first home defeat for exactly six months.

Somehow I could not feel despondant. The progress made by the team outweighed the results. Yes, we had suffered badly with injuries and suspensions, but overall I was nowhere near as depressed as I had been at this stage last season. I have a lot of faith in Aize and what he is doing. I hope he proves me correct.

Mark Aizlewood interviewed after the Airbus game

AUTUMN

The week leading up to the match against Port Talbot Town had seen constant rain fall all over South West Wales. The League Cup game at Bryntirion had been called off twice due to a waterlogged pitch and I had grave doubts about our Friday night fixture.

Gareth Jones joined me on the journey along the motorway and we watched the spray being thrown over vehicles as they sped along the western carriageway opposite. On arrival at the Victoria Road ground my trusty vehicle (only one piece of bodywork damage so far in the seven months of my ownership: reversing into a bollard at a supermarket in Brecon) was ushered into its usual space behind the main stand.

As we walked around the top of the banking towards the changing rooms the pools of water were getting larger by the minute. Once we were under shelter we could look at the pitch: it was in perfect condition and completely playable. In the away changing area there were muffled laughs when it was announced that the manager was stuck in traffic and would be late arriving. "Is he going to fine himself?" was one sympathetic comment.

Having obtained all the team information I needed I went into the clubhouse and met the usual contingent of Carmarthen's loyal followers. One duly told me of the Academy team's amazing 6-4 victory the previous evening away at Cambrian & Clydach where the lead had changed hands on a number of occasions.

Gary Morris

Fortunately on a night such as this the glass-enclosed pressbox was perfect for the three of us in occupation. I joined Matthew Burgess and Rob Clement for an evening in which we all helped each other. It is an ideal situation for at any one time one of us is watching the field of play while the others can write or broadcast. This means that nothing gets missed.

The early stages of the game had us wondering out loud as to how long it would be before referee Bryn Markham-Jones showed the first red card. In the first twenty minutes there were eleven fouls, most of which were fairly innocuous, and the showing of three yellow cards. I had seen this referee only three days earlier at Haverfordwest County and thought he had handled the match superbly. Now, with an assessor watching him, the cards were being waved.

At half-time the opinion was that the teams were cancelling each other out and this view carried on until halfway through the second period when the Old Gold were awarded a penalty following a foul on Liam McCreesh. Leon Jeanne duly converted and Carmarthen held the lead for eight minutes until a soaring shot from Port Talbot's Carl Payne flew into the top right corner of the net with Steve Cann totally beaten.

In the eightieth minute came the incident which changed the game. Payne took a melodramatic fall in the Carmarthen penalty area. It was clear that he had been watching the antics of far too many continental players as the dive set us all laughing in the pressbox. As referee Markham-Jones reached into his pocket for a yellow card so some of the players had a rather heated exchange. Cann ran from his goal, intent on getting involved in something which did not concern him, and proceeded to weigh into a group of players. The fourth official saw him trying to throttle a home defender and so it was "goodnight Steve, see you back after a three match suspension."

Richard Whalley

Jonathan Hood took over the goalkeeping duties but had no chance three minutes later when, after making a good save, the ball rebounded to Port Talbot's Lee John who just tapped the ball home. Another defeat and only two points from a possible twenty-one meant that Mark Aizlewood was a somewhat frustrated manager following the final whistle.

After he had had time to reflect we put together a Press Release in which he demanded at least five points from the following three matches. Mark insisted that the record must improve quickly. "I knew things would not be easy after signing a virtually new squad at the beginning of the season," he said. "I was at pains to point out to anybody who would listen that this process was going to take time. This is proving to be the case."

He continued: "On a more positive note we are now considerably better off in terms of points than at the same stage last season. In every league any team which finishes second from bottom one season finds it difficult to have a complete turnaround the next."

Aizlewood concluded by saying: "Neil Smothers and I remain convinced that the way we are running the club and the standards we are setting will ensure improvements. Once the consistency in performance is achieved then success can be sustained." In support of this view John Collyer, writing in the *Carmarthen Journal*, stated 'that while results during this poor run have been depressing, the performances in many games have been more encouraging.'

It wasn't all bad over the weekend as the Reserves defeated Garden Village 4-3, with Richard Whalley grabbing two more goals to add to his season's total. The Academy played a League Cup tie against Port Talbot Town on the first Sunday of October losing 2-1 in a tightly fought encounter.

On the following Tuesday the much postponed Welsh Premier League Cup tie at Bryntirion finally got under way. Only three of the former starting line-up took part and it was one of the previous Friday's substitutes, Liam Thomas, who scored both goals in a 2-1 win over the Welsh League club. Waiting for Carmarthen in the next round were Port Talbot Town so, no doubt, we will be continuing our now regular friendly encounters.

Forty-eight hours later two player movements took place. Jack Christopher returned to Haverfordwest County and we took twenty year old Scott Quigley on loan for a month from The New Saints. In some ways I felt sorry for Jack. I had always found him a pleasant fellow but often wondered why the previous manager had signed him. He did not fit in with the style of play then, nor did he now under the Aizlewood/Smothers coaching regime. In reality his stay at the club had been numbered for some time.

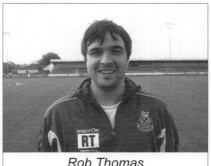

Rob Thomas

During the week I had been quite ill and, when on the mend, felt that some fresh air was needed. So the decision was made to go for a walk around some of the local area to see what places of interest could be found. Knowing that Carmarthen Town had been formed in July 1950 by Jack Harding, I paid a pilgrimage to the Penllwyn Park ground which the club used for their first two seasons.

Situated behind Picton Terrace, virtually in a straight line north from the Picton Monument, the ground is still used for community recreation. However, any signs of it having hosted Carmarthenshire League football have long since disappeared. I wonder if we should erect a plaque to commemorate our founding home?

The next league game was at Richmond Park against newly promoted Connah's Quay. Their two year absence from the WPL had been quite unjust for they failed the cut by goal difference when the size of the league had been reduced and then refused promotion from the Cymru Alliance on the most fragile of technicalities. Now they were back in their rightful place.

The rain had poured down overnight and initially I had been concerned about the state of the pitch. From early morning Jonathan Lewis, aided by Andrew Thomas, had been working to dry the surface as best as they could and also to make sure the line markings were acceptable.

Ninety minutes before the start the pitch looked perfect. The visitors had a light workout while Mark was putting the Carmarthen players through their paces. I snatched a quick chat with Scott Quigley while taking photographs of him for use by the local newspaper and the club's website. He was a pleasant lad who was keen to get onto the pitch to see some action.

Pam Davies

The Old Gold started at a terrific rate with shots from all angles and the woodwork rattled but it was Connah's Quay who took the lead ten minutes before half-time. At the break Aizlewood decided to makes some changes. "I could have left things as they were," he said later, "but I felt that we needed a radical change so risking a heavier defeat in the process."

"Ironically, the change worked perfectly. We got our noses in front at 2-1 within ten minutes of the restart but before I had a chance to re-organise we conceded a second goal only two minutes after taking the lead." He then changed the tactics to an attacking formation by putting three men up front which rather left the defence exposed. However, two breakaway goals gave the visitors the match 4-2 and all three points.

After the game a number of spectators climbed the steps to where I was sitting and there was quite an informal debate. No one made any personal criticisms of the manager: their real gripe was the team's defence. Most spoke about one particular frailty (which was a repeat of the criticism of last season's occupier of the position) and how it could be resolved.

In the following Wednesday's edition of the *Carmarthen Journal* Aizlewood was quoted as saying: "Coach Neil Smothers, General Manager Kevin Morris and I have complete faith in the players we brought in during a very busy summer period, and we have belief in the ability they have. It is just a matter of time until the club starts an upward movement in the league."

Still, it was not all gloom and doom as the excellent Academy side had travelled to Aberaman and beaten Aberdare Town 8-1 with Sam Wilson getting four of them.

As I left the ground Willy Thomas gave me a sheaf of papers to read. They were his treasures and I was touched that he trusted me enough to let me take them home. Later in the evening I went through them and there was one constant theme in all of the press cuttings, which dated back some twenty years or so, and that concerned the club's finances.

At the dawn of the League of Wales (LOW) a number of clubs from around the Principality had expressed their doubts as to the viability of the concept. The then General Secretary (later to be Chief Executive) of the Football Association of Wales, Alun Evans, had pushed through the formation of the league even though he later suffered defeat in the courts when a number of clubs playing in the English non-league system challenged his decision.

Michelle Hopkins

I am proud to say that I knew Alun quite well and following retirement he studied for his Masters degree. Not only did he pass with flying colours but his dissertation on the culture of Welsh International Football won him a distinction. He went on to study for a Doctorate of Philosophy but had to curtail it when the illness, which would finally take his life, struck him down.

We spent many hours talking about the LOW and nowhere in our discussions can I remember the subject of club finances being raised. Alun was convinced that the teams which comprised the league would always be self sufficient representatives of the country as a whole. There was no way he could ever have envisaged what has happened in that no team from Cardiff is represented.

After the Connah's Quay match the WPL table had the five North Wales teams on top; the three Mid-Wales sides astride the league cut-off line; and all four South Wales clubs in the relegation half. Of these last four, Llanelli are in desperate financial trouble.

With UEFA and WPL licensing standards being so strict it is no wonder that so few clubs outside of the WPL wish to apply for promotion. In the south only Haverfordwest County can meet the stringent rules and even then they are not sure if they can afford the jump. Cefn Druids in North Wales have previously passed the grading with a northern group of Porthmadog, Rhyl and Llandudno ready at the moment with others waiting in the wings.

The reality is that should a team from the south drop out (as Neath did last season) then the space would be filled by a club from the north. Let this happen for a couple more years and who knows what the ridiculously small twelve team league will look like.

Clubs along the North Wales coast have easy access to players from Liverpool, Manchester and other north-westerly parts of England. Some of them have the finances to offer good money to those playing in far higher standard leagues than the WPL. In the south it is completely the opposite: money is tight; players are offered only a percentage of the money of their Northern counterparts; while their standard of play is, in general terms, about two levels lower. It is not an even playing field.

Gwyn Derfel and Jeff Thomas

I mused over this dilemma for a few days, looking at the realities as it concerned Carmarthen Town Football Club. We have a first-team, most of whom travel considerable distances to train and to play in home matches; a reserve side who play in the Second Division of the Carmarthenshire League; an Academy side who are the equal of those in the Western division (but not the Eastern Division) of the Welsh Youth League, and three under age sides.

Then you have the managerial and coaching side of the first-team, all of whom are based at the eastern end of the Welsh part of the M4. No wonder, for away matches, our regular meeting point is in Rhayader as it is the easiest place for most people to reach when travelling north.

Next to consider is the cost of running a team in the WPL. This season's budget is under six figures of which about five-percent comes from the league (with another grant specifically earmarked for the Academy). So where does this money come from? The answer is from sponsors and fund-raising. In these dire economic times the amount being donated from sponsors gets less each season.

In Carmarthen we are fortunate in that not only are we a county town but, by far, the largest settlement in South-West Wales. This has attracted quality retail outlets, as has been seen by the enormous town centre redevelopment which, in itself, has attracted shoppers from a wide area. Retailers need to be recognised and promoting yourself through a sporting outlet is one of the ways to accomplish this aim.

However, should things get worse then an advertising / sponsorship budget is the first to be hit, and where would that leave the football club? Even the coach hire at around £600 a time would be difficult to find. So what is the solution?

The answer is unpalatable to those who love the club playing in the WPL, even if it does mean fixtures against the same side up to seven times in a season as happened to Port Talbot Town and Afan Lido last year. A drop down to the First Division of the Welsh League is the key to resolving the financial pressures.

I had to exercise my mind as to the repercussions of such a situation. Would the income stream from Vice-Presidents and season-ticket holders be reduced by much? Would sponsors desert us in droves? Would pay-at-the-gate attendances fall even lower than they are at the moment? Would all grants cease to be awarded? All seem unanswerable.

Willy Thomas

But what of the benefits? Certainly we would be a big fish in a small pond. There would be little doubt that we would win far more games than we have done in recent seasons and, if so, would this attract the general public as spectators who like to be associated with success instead of constant failure. Would winning make everybody connected with the club any happier? Who knows.

On the Friday evening before our trip to Newtown I went to see Llanelli play Afan Lido. It was a splendidly enjoyable contest and, as a neutral, I was

45

caught up in the atmosphere as Llanelli scored three times in the last few minutes to win the game.

But it was the little things which were noticeable and at half-time I spoke about them with Monro Walters who has been the ground announcer at the club for many years. It all started when we were in the boardroom and noticed that the usual hospitality had been reduced to a packet of tea-bags and a jar of coffee. Over the years I have found that this unusual gauge of a club's diminishing finances has always proved to be correct.

Then we realised that there had been no half-time draw for a raffle prize and that the usual faces had not come among the crowd selling tickets during the first-half. The matchday programme had halved in price as the pages had been reduced to the minimum number allowed by the WPL and, of course, there was no Nigel Richards as the former General Manager had been made redundant. It was all very sad.

Monro was blunt with his opinion. "I just hope that the club survives," he said. "I think that the main fear people have is that we will go the same way as Neath and just fold. We know that we are not going to get a UEFA licence for next season and the way things are at present we won't even get a WPL domestic licence. All I can look forward to is that we will be able to start a new life in the Welsh League."

I kept reflecting on Monro's words as I was driven north to Newtown the following morning. As my wife was driving she had little option but to listen to my worries about the future of the game in our part of the world.

Latham Park is situated on the southern end of the town just up from the banks of the River Severn. It is a delightful ground with glorious views of the surrounding hills. While my wife went shopping with relatives (usually a costly exercise) I, along with others from Carmarthen, was invited to join the Newtown committee for lunch.

As the match was being televised the usual Saturday afternoon timing schedules are disrupted as the later kick-off is arranged to fit in with S4C's broadcasting timetable. From my point of view this meant varied radio reports and never a final summary as most sports programmes have gone off the air before the final whistle sounds.

I spread my papers along the top of the pressbox, which is situated at the back of one of the stands, and waited for the start. It took just seven minutes for the action to begin when Mark Aizlewood was sent from the dugout to the stand by referee Lee Evans.

It started when Jonathan Hood was fouled near to the dugout. Aizlewood queried with referee Evans as to why a yellow card had not been shown to the offending Newtown player. According to Aizlewood the answer was: "Yes, I know it was worthy of a card but only seven minutes have gone and, anyway, we are live on television."

The Carmarthen Town manager replied that a card should be shown at any time. He was told to keep quiet but reiterated his view and was sent off. As Mark said later: "I have been sent from the dugout three times in my thirty year coaching career and they have all been in live television games."

However, the fun was only just starting. Frustrated at standing on the bottom step of the stand, Aize asked fourth official Nick Pratt if he could position himself behind the dugout. Permission was granted until referee Evans spotted it and gave instructions for him to move back to the stand.

Mark did so for a few minutes and then got Equipment Manager Gareth Davies to ask Pratt if he could go around to the stand on the far side of the ground. Permission granted. Aize trotted around, took up his new position and started bellowing out instructions.

Referee Evans, during a stoppage in play, instructed two burly stewards to escort Aizlewood back to his original sending-off point. On seeing what was happening Gareth Jones went to help out and to bring our frustrated manager back to his originally designated place.

Sent to the Stand at Newtown

By this time there were virtually tears of laughter from the spectators in the seats near to me at the antics being carried on while the match was in progress, but there was still more to come. Aize stood on the bottom step and continued bawling tactical directions to his players. Still not happy, referee Evans sent instructions for him to go further back up the stand. Aize moved to a halfway point.

A few minutes later the decent fourth official (who kept apologising to the visitor's bench for the farce) received instructions to get Aize to go right to the back of the stand. From there he had a perfect view of the pitch and for the rest of the game his loud voice could be heard above everything else in the ground. It was all very comical.

On the field the injury Hood had received in the tackle which started the farce had proved too much and he was substituted. Then Leon Jeanne retired from the fray and Aize threw on Julian Alsop, a cult hero amongst many at the club.

By now the Old Gold were a goal down but at the interval the manager made a tactical change which turned the course of the afternoon. He moved Alsop forward and the experienced journeyman footballer proved his manager correct. For the whole of the second-half Alsop worried the Newtown defence so much that they spent their time watching him rather than the ball. From the pressbox it was wonderful to see an old professional in action.

Casey Thomas came on as a substitute with twenty minutes left and scored with his first touch; a fierce drive from thirty yards into the bottom left corner of the Newtown net. Two minutes later, as the defence followed Alsop, Liam Thomas moved clear of his defender and crashed the ball home.

Afterwards, Aizlewood said: "The spirit and character of my players made me a very proud man. They came through against all odds to win us a really valuable three points. We started the day unable to select six first choice players through a combination of injury and suspension. To compound this, we then had to make two first-half substitutions due to further injuries."

Ifor Hughes

However, there was one person the manager had to mention. "It is not usual for me to single out an individual player for praise but on this occasion I feel it is appropriate to do so. Julian Alsop was pressed into emergency service an hour prior to the start and, for someone who had not played competitive football for eight months, he became an unbelievable influence on the game."

"Julian is thirty-nine years old; has played in nearly eight hundred senior matches, and is now in his twenty-third season. We practically had to carry him up the steps to the changing room after the game as he could hardly walk, but what an example he was to our young players with his attitude and enthusiasm."

"There really is something special about his positioning and pivotal edge, with his distribution being near perfect. He has become an instant hero with our group of players and who knows what role he will play from here on in."

It really is fascinating what a win does, not only for the morale of the team, but also for the club officials and supporters. There was suddenly a spring in the step of the Carmarthen followers and the Newtown club bar was far louder at the end of the afternoon than it had been at half-time. In the car-park I saw Matthew Rees, Jonathan Hood and Craig Hanford, and congratulated them all on a fine performance. I knew they were proud by their slightly embarrassed thanks in return.

While all this was going on the club's Reserves had won at home defeating Swiss Valley 3-1 with Richard Whalley scoring his twenty-second goal of the season.

The following afternoon the Academy side took on Afan Lido in the second round of the Football Association of Wales Youth Cup. As always Peter Fearn's team entertained and I sat in the stand along with Andrew Thomas admiring the quality of some of the play. Like Aize I try not to pick out any player but the quality of Iestyn Evans' performance shone through like a beacon.

It was his spectacular thirty-five yard free kick which gave Carmarthen the lead but goals from the visitors either side of the break made defeat a possibility. Ten minutes from time Peter changed the formation and almost immediately Callum Jackson equalised. Then, with just three minutes left, a curling corner was neatly headed in by central-defender Gavin Rees to claim an excellent victory and a home tie in the next round.

Monday 22 October saw yet another Extra Ordinary General Meeting. This time it was to fill the remaining vacant Director's position and to go through suggestions for the re-writing of the club's constitution. There were quite a number of matters which needed to be voted upon and, strangely, the gathering was anything but boring and stilted. The attendance was good and everybody joined in with an opinion.

Aizlewood interviewed at Newtown

The evening seemed to be a catalyst for me for suddenly my diary was getting full with the dates of meetings; press releases to write and distribute; emails to send round and people to see. Where did my quiet retirement go to?

The next day was anything but quiet as Danny Thomas announced his retirement from WPL football. He had accepted a position with the Cardiff City Academy which meant that he was unable to train with us nor could he travel to away games. In an emergency he could play at home but his fitness levels might not be as high as required. Then goalkeeper Rhys Wilson was transferred to Taff's Well and the following day Anthony Finselbach moved down the road to Haverfordwest County. All needed press releases to be prepared and sent out. I'm looking forward to the weekend match and a bit of a rest.

Julian Alsop

The weather had turned cold and on my way to our match against Aberystwyth I stopped in Aberaeron to visit a bookshop. The biting wind from Cardigan Bay nearly froze me as I battled to get into the warmth. For some reason the town was very busy: I presume the second-home owners were having a half-term break. Certainly the accents were very different: the young girls especially with their upper-crust home-counties public-school voices.

On arriving at the Park Avenue ground I was unofficially told about the contents of the referee's report from last Saturday when Mark was sent to the stand. Later, he told me himself what the report contained. Now, I have been around the football world for a number of decades and am very much aware of these things. I am sure Lee Evans is a very nice fellow and he is loved by his family. However, his comments about the words and actions used by Aize were not those I had actually heard and seen. But, like all such clashes the officials are right and everyone else is wrong. As Aize said: "To appeal will cost £600, so why bother, we'll only lose."

The Carmarthen line-up for the match showed four changes from the winning side at Newtown. Steve Cann and Liam McCreesh were back from suspension; Carl Evans from injury and Julian Alsop was starting as an old-fashioned centre-forward. Also the formation was changed from the 4-4-1-1 we had been using to 4-3-3. This, to me, was a clear statement of intent.

Before the start Aneurin Venables, the home media officer, and I had to give our respective match previews: him to *Radio Ceredigion* and mine to *Radio Carmarthenshire*. However, the amusing thing was that we both were contacted by the same producer and our reports followed each other. But, then again, he had his local angle and I had mine.

As there is no pressbox at Park Avenue I sat at the front of the elevated stand with John Collyer and we watched a first-half which was totally controlled by

Carmarthen who were going forward into a very strong wind. After the break nothing changed until just after the hour mark when a deflected shot hit the knee of Craig Hanford and looped agonisingly over the head of Steve Cann. We knew then that there would be no more goals.

Afterwards the management trio of Mark, Neil Smothers and Kevin Morris were virtually speechless. The team had done everything asked of them and they had nothing to show for it. "Aberystwyth will never get a luckier three points," said Aize as we walked to his car. "Never."

Back at Richmond Park the Reserves had chalked up another big win, this time 8-0 over Penyfan which stretched their lead at the top of the league. The following afternoon the Academy side lost 2-0 at Port Talbot Town in a league fixture having had their only previous defeat of the season at the same ground in a cup match.

On the Tuesday evening we played Port Talbot Town in the quarter-final of the League Cup competition. Although it was slightly cold I started wondering if anyone was going to turn up as there were just a few hardy souls sitting in the stand ten minutes prior to the start. Eventually more arrived, many of them students from the nearby college, and the final attendance was given as 147. To add insult to injury only thirteen programmes were sold and the ladies did not arrive to open the tea-bar.

Peter Fearn

The multi-media centre would have been a lonely place had I not been joined by Jonathan and Willy. We were virtually speechless as Port Talbot scored after two minutes with a header from a corner. Five minutes later an attempted clearance by Steve Cann somehow ended up in the back of his net. Two goals down and eighty-three minutes to go: was it going to get any worse?

Soon the Carmarthen defence started to tighten. Iestyn Evans played superbly in the left back position while Carl Evans and Matthew Rees excelled in their central defensive roles. At the interval Aize had a quiet word (that's a joke) with the players which seemed to have an effect. They came from the changing room and started to play in the way most of us had been hoping they would.

After nine minutes Liam Thomas fired in a twenty yard shot: Eight minutes later he tapped in a squared pass from the right, and with a quarter of an hour left Liam McCreesh followed up a rebound. It was 3-2 and our little group were in a seventh heaven. It could have been more as the shots rained in on Port Talbot goalkeeper Craig Richards. Then referee Brian James blew the final whistle and we were in the semi-final to play against Llanelli.

The next morning it was confirmed that we had home advantage but the only setback was that the WPL had set the date for eight days hence. This meant getting articles organised for a programme; trying to find space in the clubhouse for visitors and guests, as a long term booking could not be changed; and informing supporters about the event taking place.

But before all that there was the Saturday home match against Airbus Broughton. Overnight the rain had fallen by the bucket-full and just after lunch dark clouds hovered over the ground. I mentioned the rain to referee Kris Hames when he arrived. "I live in Aberdare," he told me, "and my garden rain-gauge has recorded four and a half inches of rain in the past ten days."

Clive Evans

As always the pitch looked perfect and the players warm-up had no effect on it. An hour and a half before the start Aize took the players into conclave with the door locked behind them. As he said later: "Along with the coaching staff we spent an hour with the squad before the match laying out the game plan. While we did not change our usual system we changed the 'type' of player who started in certain positions to counteract the strengths of Airbus."

At half-time, with the match scoreless, a small group congregated around the press area. The opinions were all along the lines that it was a nothing game: nothing was happening. What did we poor punters know? It had been Aizlewood's plan all along to stymie the visitor's experienced attack, a fact I found out afterwards, and for the second-half to adopt completely different tactics.

It all paid off. Watching the final forty-five minutes of play who could ever have thought that the two teams were at opposite ends of the league table. The goals, when they came, were condensed into an eight minute spell in the last quarter. Two strikes from the ever improving Liam Thomas (as well as the woodwork being rattled a few times) to a tap-in goal from the visitor's forward

Steve Abbott. This was more like it.

The same faces gathered around me at the end. Most were completely stunned by the change around. Aize was not: "For us to have taken six points from Airbus in two games is a magnificent accomplishment for my club and I believe that no other team in the league will be able to achieve this feat during the season."

"While I am obviously delighted with the three points, it was the nature of the victory and the performance of the players for the full ninety minutes which gives me so much optimism for the future."

Some thirty-five or so years ago the actor and comedian John Cleese produced a short film called 'Meetings, Bloody Meetings' in which he ridiculed the need for organisations to have so many time-consuming gatherings. His wrath was mainly aimed at government departments, as I understood so well having been employed by the civil service very early in my working life. Now I appear to be back into the swing of it again as the club has a number of

Liam Thomas signing his contract

planned forthcoming events, all of which need to be properly arranged. The most important of these is the UEFA Under-19 Women's Finals' tournament which is being held in South Wales next August.

The awarding of the event was just the start. A detailed time-table had to be organised and, from a Carmarthen Town point of view, the new changing rooms, currently under construction, had to be ready in time to receive official approval.

There have already been a few necessary meetings and some initial plans have had to be revised. For example, Bridge Meadow, the home of Haverfordwest County, was originally on the venue list. However, UEFA tournament rules state that no ground will be more than an hour's drive from a team's hotel and as Swansea is the base for most participating teams then another location had to be chosen.

The morning of Guy Fawkes' Day saw my computer in-box cluttered with the details of various meetings, most of which were initiated from Cardiff by the FAW. The most important one stated: "As part of the preliminary organisational work for the Finals we need to make a further inspection visit to your ground."

It went on to list the FAW and UEFA members who would be attending, then adding: "During our three day stay we will be visiting eight training venues, five match venues and five hotels."

The detailed planning could not be faulted and Ceri Stennett's missive added: "We would need to spend time at each venue to check on all facilities and to draw up a list of any potential further work to be done or completed." By the looks of things it would appear that for the matches played before the semi-finals the venues would be us at Richmond Park, Stebonheath Park in Llanelli, Afan Lido by Aberavon Beach and the Brewery Field, Bridgend.

From the ideas being put forward the suggested semi-finals and final venue would be at Parc-y-Scarlets, Llanelli. The eight training grounds would be at clubs in Port Talbot, Swansea and Llanelli. It was going to be a busy few days. Alas, I had to send my early apologies for not taking part in this as I would be away in Scotland.

Keiran Davies

One meeting I would need to attend G.O. had scheduled for Thursday 8 November, the day of our semi-final. It was very much a preliminary UEFA get-together with representatives from the FAW, Carmarthenshire County Council, Carmarthen Town Council, Tourist Association, Managers of the two town retail centres and from the football club.

What did impress me during the meeting was the grasp of current social media resources by those promoting the town and county. Also the fact that tourist information fact-sheets had been translated into a number of languages, the latest being in Mandarin due to growing business activities with China. You really do learn something new every day.

The two hours before the evening's league cup semi-final against Llanelli were taken up with the formalities of signing twenty-one year old Liam Thomas on a long term contract. Then we had the publicity photo-shoot after which I interviewed him on video for placing on the club's website.

The Llanelli management and players did not look a happy bunch when they arrived. The previous days' edition of the *London Gazette* had announced that yet again HM Revenue & Customs had issued a winding-up order against the club for unpaid taxes. Where will it end?

Mark Aizlewood had sent me the evening's team earlier in the day and followed it up with a 'phone call to talk about possible late match tactical changes. Knowing what had happened in games over the past few weeks I doubted if his original ideas would see fruit. They didn't, as Carl Evans was injured in the first-half and coaching decisions had to be made on the spot as appropriate.

While our little group around the media centre scoffed my wife's home-made biscuits, Llanelli made the early running. The danger signs came after a quarter of an hour when defender Chris Thomas slammed a shot against the Carmarthen crossbar with the home defence looking rattled. Three minutes later Antonio Corbisiero put the visitors in front.

Nowadays the Old Gold do not drop their heads: Aize has trained them well. It took only twelve minutes for Casey Thomas to score a spectacular thirty-yard special into the top right corner of Llanelli's net and from then on it was only going to be a matter of time before the winning goal arrived.

At each match the *'Julian Alsop Fan Club'* congregate behind whichever goal Carmarthen are attacking. They chant their hero's name, even when he is not playing. Tonight all their dreams came true as, twenty minutes from time, their hero rose high above the visitors' defence to put his team into January's final against The New Saints.

Cordelia Evans and Olga Williams

After the joyous on-field scenes following the final whistle I walked back around the ground to the matchday office. As Huw Davies said: "Isn't it amazing how a win puts a smile back on people's faces."

It was more than smiles. It was four wins out of five; the first time we had defeated Llanelli in fourteen attempts; a first cup final appearance in eight years, and a complete turnaround since the unmitigated disaster of this time last year. Then came the news that Matthew Rees had won the WPL Player-of-the-Month Award.

Can it get much better?

Matthew Rees receiving the
WPL Player of the Month Award

| Nicky Palmer | Liam Thomas | Kerry Nicholas | Tim Hicks |
| Liam McCreesh | Sam Wilson | Casey Thomas | Craig Hughes |

THE RUN UP TO CHRISTMAS

The middle Saturday in November had been designated by chairman Neil Alexander as 'Pink Day.' The match against Prestatyn Town was going to be televised as a live game and so it would give the club an excellent opportunity to raise money for charitable purposes as well as getting considerable publicity.

On the previous Wednesday training had taken place, as usual, in 'The Barn' although it had started late due to the presence of Arwyn Williams from Rondo Media who was filming the session for broadcasting before the match started. The pink shirts duly arrived from the manufacturer for the players to wear during filming and a photo-shoot. Suddenly someone realised that the shirts had no squad numbers on the back so they were quickly returned the next morning to be embossed.

In the half an hour between when everyone arrived and filming started the players gathered in their usual corner to change and to pass the time of day. I had brought along a copy of the *Carmarthen Journal* for Mark Aizlewood to read what had been printed in the latest issue about him and the club. A few of the players read the articles and I mentioned to some of them as to how the quotes were obtained and put into the context they were reading.

Neil Alexander

The younger members of the squad were polite enough to listen to my warbling and occasionally asked a question. What did take me back was the belligerence shown by a couple of the more senior players whose cynicism made me feel that they had had a bad press at previous clubs. As a whole most of the squad are quite self effacing so maybe it is possible the odd one or two like to fight shy, or are very nervous, of publicity.

The Saturday morning of the Prestatyn game was hectic, to put it mildly. Everyone seemed to have a job to do and the ground was bustling with people. A big chunk of the Priory Street car-park was occupied by television vans and although I arrived four hours before the start I was fortunate enough to get the final parking space.

The matchday office was a hive of activity and all of us were caught up in the buzz. I find it fascinating how most of the club's officials seem to know what to do at any time especially on a day when the needs of the television crew take priority. So that I did not stuff up my role I had prepared a list giving detail of the time of each radio broadcast, photo-shoot and interview during the afternoon. Almost immediately Emyr James, my radio producer, rang to say the programme schedule for the game had changed and gave me new times. So, it was an immediate reorganisation of the day.

My wife had baked cupcakes for the charity day and topped them with piles of pink tinted butter-icing and pink coated smarties. The first tin became empty before I had even unpacked my bags, so much for the alleged comments of: "I must restrain myself before lunch." The other tins were immediately removed to the media centre.

G.O. & Arwyn Williams filming for Sgorio

Gareth Davies had set out the pink kit in the changing room with the named shirts hanging from the players' pegs. All went well until Carl Evans shirt was unpacked and there, on the back, was 'K.Evans.' I don't think it sold at the post-match auction. As I took various photographs so Gareth was able to hide the rogue 'K' which meant that within the hour they were all available for webmaster Huw Davies to upload and no one could have spotted the error.

In an idle few minutes I was able to chat with WPL Secretary Gwyn Derfel about his time at the BBC and how reporting had changed since my voice first hit the airwaves back in 1969 (writing that has really made me feel old!). Then it was into the clubhouse for a photographic montage of the guests before they sat down to lunch. I asked Michelle Hopkins about the menu and her detailed reply made me feel very hungry.

The two *Sgorio* presenters, John Hartson and Malcolm Allen, were preparing themselves for their first broadcast when Hartson was called away. This left me with Malcolm and we spent the time reminiscing about the days we were both at Millwall, albeit with me in the pressbox. I found it quite amazing that we could both speak in some detail about a match played at Fratton Park against Portsmouth back in 1991, and the incidents which caused the then manager to lose his job forty-eight hours later.

Players in Pink

The media centre did not have many of the club's supporters sitting nearby as is usually the case. The town's car-parks were all full which would not have helped and with the late afternoon kick-off and live television coverage many would have stayed in the warmth of their own homes. However, this did not stop the cakes being scoffed on a regular basis by those who braved the elements.

The match had everything. After four minutes Julian Alsop was hit in the face and shortly afterwards was dismissed for retaliation. Later Mark Aizlewood reflected on a rumbustious game and what he considered to be referee Lee Evans' incorrect decisions at critical moments. "When Prestatyn goalkeeper Jon Hill-Dunt brought down Liam Thomas after ten minutes it was an obvious red-card decision as confirmed by television replays. But only a yellow was shown. Then Casey Thomas was brought down in the area, again with television proving the foul, but no action was taken. In addition, Prestatyn's Jason Price committed a deliberate hand-ball for a penalty and, in my opinion, this should also have warranted a red card."

Poor Aize. At Carmarthen's last televised game the same referee had sent him to the stand (fortunately it was only a mild fine from the FAW) and now all this. Never mind; with other incidents happening elsewhere we soon became aware that even with Jules' sending-off Carmarthen had

Filming in the Barn

risen from the bottom of the Fair Play League.

The ninety minutes of play were pulsating and given the league positions of the clubs a 2-2 draw would have been accepted before the start. But that would not have told the full story by any means. Aize could hardly contain his admiration and pride when interviewed later for *Sgorio*: "The biggest compliment you can give to my players is that after conceding a goal in the fifth minute of added time at the end of the game, it felt like a defeat."

He added: "All of them were desperately disappointed when they returned to the changing room. However, I was at pains to point out that we had just dominated Prestatyn for eighty-five minutes with ten men on the field; a team which had been in the top two positions of the league all season."

The feeling in the matchday office was one of immense pride that the players had given such a momentous performance on what had been an important day for the club. Chairman Neil Alexander felt that the whole day had been a wonderful advertisement for the club which had also been enjoyed by a television audience. Even the Prestatyn players were sporting enough to mention that they had been very fortunate to gain a point.

John Hartson, Gwyn Derfel and Malcolm Allen

The whole day had been a credit to all concerned. All I could hope was that the next match, away in Oswestry, would not be an after-the-Lord-Mayor's-Show event and fall absolutely flat.

Two days later the long awaited release by the Welsh Assembly's *'Communities, Equality and Local Government Committee's'* report into the Welsh Premier League saw the fifty-one page document fall into my in-tray. I was hoping to be surprised by the odd rogue recommendation but was rather disappointed. The issues which dominated the meeting of the Committee which I attended in Llanelli were not addressed as "they came outside our Terms of Reference."

There was a considerable amount of 'playing to the Gallery' and immense 'political correctness' within the pages as well as a prominence given to matters favoured by football administrators but considerably unpopular with most of the clubs and their fans.

Then again, I just loved the nonsensical jargon. We had "Hub models," an "equality angle," a "BME background," a "strategy to outline its vision," or to "support the delivery of broader policy objectives." I did like the quotes "this sort of spend," and "constructive relationships," along with "optimise the standards," generic "prioritise" on numerous suggestions and the always wonderful "joined up approaches."

I have a one thousand page modern dictionary and I could find none of the above used in this form. My only answer would be to get a group of bright A-level standard English language students together, hand over copies of this report and ask them to translate it into a readable form. I wonder if they would succeed?

What did annoy me was the blatant way in which football administrators had pushed the party bandwagon with so called 'facts' which were exactly the opposite of those expressed by people who had either attended the open meetings or sent in written submissions. Even the Committee noted this in the preface to some submission quotations used in the report.

That night we had a Management Committee meeting in the clubhouse and G.O. asked if I would mind going through this report as well as the FAW response and the WPL Strategy paper, both of which had been handed out at the previous day's WPL Chairmen's meeting.

John Hartson, Malcolm Allen and Neil Alexander

I willingly agreed and in the preface to what I presented stated: "I have, over the years, been familiar with similar papers prepared by The [English] Football Association and have written articles on them. These include the infamous 1991 document which stated that the then proposed Premier League, to replace the old First Division, 'would not work;' quote Graham Kelly (FA Secretary)."

I looked first at the National Assembly Report and observed: 'The committee findings into the WPL is typical of any government report in that it tries not to offend by using excess verbiage. If it had been prepared for use by private enterprise it would have been around twenty pages. The submissions made before, during and after the report's findings were known have been made by people who are answerable to higher authority and therefore they have had to toe the party line whether they believed what they said, or not. The errors of both fact and perceived opinion by the FAW and WPL representatives have given the report an official gloss which is not deserved. On the other hand, at least twenty of the twenty-eight independent submissions state fact and opinion widely held by the clubs and their supporters.'

By now I was getting into my stride. 'However, there is one very major point which the committee failed to appreciate and that is the *standard* of skill and play in the WPL compared to elsewhere. It is my view, and that of many others, that the level of WPL football equals what is known as Level 7/8 in England, or to convert to the non-league criteria, Steps 3/4. The North Wales clubs are generally Step 3 (Southern/Northern Premier Leagues) while generally Mid and South Wales clubs are Step 4. A recent study by the sports science department at Loughborough University, using parallel frame-by-frame slow-motion analysis confirms this view.'

The report then looked at G.O's excellent submission (which I detailed in the second chapter) and the FAW's reply which did not address any of Gareth's issues in a proper manner but sought to praise the FAW Council. I thought it was a masterpiece in grovelling.

In its next section the Committee moved on to look at the relationship between the FAW and the WPL clubs. The introduction talked about the supporters, who attended the two public meetings, feeling that the FAW and its strategies were completely irrelevant to them. The report added: "There was clearly a sense of disaffection amongst those we spoke to. There is a

Dylan Ebenezer, Malcolm Allen and John Hartson

lot of work to be done by the FAW to build relationships between it and the clubs. While the FAW strategies are impressive and ambitious on paper they will not succeed if they don't take the clubs and their fans with them." My obvious question to the above points is: 'Who from the FAW and WPL have ever come to the clubs to tell us this?

I'm afraid I was somewhat blunt with my assessment of the following paragraph: "The FAW needs to prioritise communication and relationship building with the clubs." Yes - and pigs might fly. The only time we see the majority of FAW officials at the club is usually the 42nd minute of the first-half when they are running to be first in the queue for the complimentary tea and sandwiches. Talk to the punters? Have *you* ever tried to engage with an FAW councillor? I have, on three occasions, and each time have been treated with an air of contempt.

Now the Report moved on to my area of speciality: The Media and its coverage of the WPL. The Welsh newspaper industry is slated for its lack of interest in the league and I commented: "Let's be truly honest with each other here: if I was a South Wales newspaper's sports editor with two Premiership clubs and one top Football Conference club on my doorstep where do you think I would aim my coverage? Top football sells newspapers and surely you would fill your allocated space with what most punters want to read. Do readers in Newport, Cardiff and Swansea really want to know about clubs who are nowhere near to them?

In a very telling comment in the Report, the Sport Wales submission stated, about media coverage, "if you had representatives of women's sports here they would have even greater complaints about non-coverage than the WPL."

In response the FAW replied as follows (and don't laugh out loud when you read this): "We have made significant strides and changed fundamentally the way in which football is reported in this country across all levels in all the media." To make things worse, the WPL agreed. Have you ever read such self-serving nonsense? Then it got worse. The WPL stated that since a twelve team league came into being "gates have increased by 26%." Our own John Collyer, who writes match reports for the *Carmarthen Journal*, has compiled figures which show a completely opposite trend.

In discussing the WPL's twelve-team format, the submission from the Secretary stated: "The bold introduction of the format has led to more meaningful and exciting football [and increased spectator interest]." However, the Committee reported that 'most of the clubs who provided evidence did not agree that the system was working,' adding 'that the amount of times the clubs play each other in a season is too many, leading to lower attendances and a lack of interest.'

Hartson & Allen

The public meetings were strong in their views calling the new format "a disaster" and a "complete travesty."

In reply to these criticisms the WPL argued about familiarity in teams playing each other up to seven times a season by stating: "We have revamped the league cup [by including four teams from each of the Welsh League and Cymru Alliance] .... to try and engage the feeder-league clubs to aspire to come to the national league." To which I commented: "Really? An attendance of 58 at Haverfordwest; with double figures at northern matches? Who on earth are you trying to fool?

The Report then moved on to talk about 'Player and Coach Development.' The FAW's Technical Director told the Committee that the WPL: "Can produce talent, and produce them regularly, who can be sold for six-figure transfer sums, the money obtained benefitting our clubs." This is blue-sky thinking on a massive scale. He added: "I think we have up to three managers in the WPL who are ready to step up." Up to where? The English Premier League? This is fanciful stuff.

But it got into more fantasy-land football when it was put to the Committee that the WPL clubs should run up to five teams each to become "developmental clubs like Barcelona and Real Madrid."

Well, that all set my blood-pressure on an upward spiral. The Committee reported faithfully on what they had heard and read, and I can only commend them for their work. I then turned to the WPL Strategy paper which was of little interest as it contained merely plans of internal discussions and liaison with the FAW Council members.

However, the FAW's reply to the Committee's report appeared to me to be a defence of any made or perceived criticism and offered replies which seemed to contradict fact and general opinion.

Dealing with the matter of communication it was stated: "The FAW currently undertakes research with clubs and supporters." Then they added, "that this research among fans is about their opinions of 'the competition format'." This, of course, would be news to the people concerned. Has anyone we know ever chatted to a researcher from the FAW? I did ask around the club after one match but the only replies I received are not fit for publication.

Then they state: "The WPL and the FAW should develop a strategy to address the lack of media coverage and the lack of attendance at matches." This latter point is a clear contradiction of what was said in submission to the Committee. In addition: "If the league continues to be starved of coverage from the main media outlets in Wales then the Welsh Government and the FAW should work together in partnership in reminding them of their responsibilities." What a beauty. So I, as a sports editor, get a delegation coming to me to tell me what I should put in my newspaper. The reply would be of two words.

The summary finished with a lovely civil service comment: "Whilst recognising the time constraints on FAW staff ....." Love it.

I must say with all respect that the Members of the Welsh Assembly who formed this committee have tried their best to get to the root of the problems surrounding the FAW and, more especially, the WPL. One of their main recommendations has been to encourage clubs to invest in 3/4G pitches. They looked closely at the Domestic Licensing system; summer football; the academies and coaching; and management structures.

However, all the time they were being fed bullshit and bluster from the FAW and WPL. As previously mentioned I attended the Llanelli open meeting and the committee chairwoman, Ann Jones, intimated quite clearly that she knew this was the case. However, the committee listened to the views put forward which, I gather, were more vociferous at the Llandudno open meeting.

What will happen to the Report? Probably very little. I cannot see much, if any, of its recommendations being implemented, certainly not in the foreseeable future. What did come out loud and clear to me was simply that the clubs must do what they are told because the FAW/WPL know what's good for them: and don't argue.

The midweek saw me in Glasgow, a city of many flavours. It is a complete opposite to Edinburgh, only an hour's drive away along the motorway, which is staid and cultured. Whereas Glasgow is unpredictable and full of surprises. I love browsing the old bookshops, many of which are hidden away in alleyways all over the western suburbs. I came back south with many new treasures.

It was an easy drive to Oswestry and my wife dropped me in the football ground's car-park just as the coach containing the Carmarthen Town team and supporters arrived. She was immediately surrounded and thanked profusely for the special cakes she had cooked which had been distributed at the previous week's match. Naturally it was Jonathan Lewis who guided the throng when asked about the flavour of the cake they would like to have for the next home game.

The Burma Road ground of TNS (full name: The New Saints of Oswestry Town & Llansantffraid Football Club) has the only 3G pitch in the WPL and it was in perfect condition for the afternoon. I set up in their splendid pressbox and the space allocated to each journalist was perfect for all of our needs. I gave my pre-match preview to *Radio Carmarthenshire* stating: "It was long ago, in February 2008, that Carmarthen Town last scored here at the Park Hall complex. Since then they have conceded twenty-eight goals. Can they hang on today?"

The feeling amongst the TNS officials in and around the press area was that the visitors had no hope of scoring especially following their 6-0 victory at

Llanelli only seven days previously. Did they want to take bets? I asked. They laughed.

Eventually the teams ran out onto the pitch. I knew the Old Gold were confident but I didn't know by how much. Aize had given eight of the team strict orders to man-mark while relying on the two front men to use their pace to get through the home defence.

After just three minutes Liam Thomas was darting through the TNS defence when he was brought down on the right edge of the penalty area. Paul Fowler stepped forward and fired sweetly into the left corner of the net. Chuckles from me: sarcasm from all around. "It won't last," said the scribe from the *Shropshire Star* newspaper.

A quarter of an hour later Casey Thomas broke free on the halfway line and sent a sublime pass to Nicky Palmer, who surged down the right wing, cut inside and from the corner of the penalty area drove the ball across goalkeeper Paul Harrison and into the net. Louder sniggers from me: outrage from the local media people.

To give them their due the TNS players had the majority of possession and territorial advantage. The statistics showed a corner count of 16-0 and Harrison only had one shot to save in the whole match. In contrast Steve Cann made save upon save to keep a blank sheet. Then came the final *coup-de-grace* when, with just fifteen minutes left, Liam McCreesh lifted a high pass over the stretched TNS defence for Liam Thomas to take the ball in his stride and crash it at an angle past Harrison.

The visiting supporters were in seventh heaven. I looked around the glum pressbox. There were long faces everywhere. The club's second lowest crowd of the season started to drift towards the exits. The score had been relayed to various results services and all of a sudden my 'phone lit up. I gave assorted reports making sure all the time that those left in the pressbox heard my glowing praise of Aize's team.

The final whistle sounded. Carmarthen's footballers had beaten the current WPL champions and league leaders on their home ground. After a few minutes respite I went down to the changing room to get Mark for a number of radio interviews. He was sitting alone on a bench. He looked mentally drained but soon got back to his normal self when a microphone was placed into his hands. For him; for the team and for the supporters this really was a victory to savour.

There were a number of interesting issues put forward at the Management Committee meeting two days later. In one, Paul Ashley-Jones gave a report on the work being done on the club's archival material which, it is hoped, in due course will be available on the clubs' website. I also put forward an idea I had regarding honouring the clubs founder and the possibility of liaising with the Carmarthen Civic Society regarding the erection of a commemorative plaque.

The first day of December dawned cold and frosty. "It was minus six degrees in Abergwili overnight," I heard one person comment as I went to get the morning newspaper. It was below freezing point mid-morning with visibility of about fifty metres and I did wonder if our game against Bala Town would go ahead.

Not only was the match played but it was one of the most dull encounters I had witnessed all season. In his match report John Collyer politely called it "a rather dour affair." He also commented that: "Matthew Rees, who had been outstanding at the heart of the defence, was shown a second yellow card for an innocuous challenge." I saw it differently, for as early as the twentieth minute I had commented to those around me that "Rees won't last the distance." The game ended 1-1, with the final whistle bringing a sigh of relief all round.

Afterwards Mark Aizlewood was furious and, as usual, quite outspoken. "I was extremely disappointed to see from the first minute of the game that the Bala Town side were encouraging the referee to caution and send off my players. As a former professional footballer myself I feel it is a cardinal sin to try and get a fellow player sent off. The visiting goalkeeper, in particular, should look closely at himself. He was constantly shouting over seventy metres to the referee at every opportunity in order to get opponents booked and shown red cards. This is a part of the game which I despise and I would never encourage any of my players to do this. What happened on the pitch left quite a lot to be desired."

Anyway, it was not all gloom as Steve 'Gas's' reserve team went to Ammanford and came away with a 2-2 draw which kept them firmly on top of the table.

It was a very quiet midweek. Mark had the idea of trying to obtain use of the Trinity College swimming pool for Wednesday's training session but permanent bookings at the time required put paid to that thought. The only paperwork I had was having to sign UEFA forms for our licensing application.

As we had been drawn away to Holyhead Hotspur in the Welsh Cup I travelled north a day early and spent the evening with friends watching Denbigh Town play in a Welsh Alliance match against Llanrwst United. The gossip turned out to be far more interesting than the game. One of the group, Leo Hoenig, spent some time telling us of his recent visit to Pyongyang to see North Korea play a World Cup qualifying match against Turkmenistan. As a very well travelled man Leo went out of his way to tell us that, in his opinion, the well publicised western view of North Korea was "somewhat over exaggerated."

I arrived at the Kingsland Road ground in Holyhead as the advance guard of the masses (that's an exaggeration, by the way) who were making their way north. A *Sgorio* camera crew were already there and we arranged times for the various filming and interviews they needed to take with the Carmarthen players and management.

A very pleasant event for me was, at long last, to meet Gareth M. Davies the Holyhead Media Officer. We had known each other for twenty years but never previously met. The friendship had developed over the telephone since the early 1990s when we had both been deeply involved in the *Association of Sports Historians*. With my knowledge of book publication I was able to guide Gareth in the writing and production of his seminal work on the history of football on the North Wales coast.

Once the television crew had obtained all they required and *Radio Carmarthenshire* had recorded a five minute preview piece, there was time to relax before kick-off. Those who had made the journey to Anglesey were G.O., Neil Alexander, Bernie Davies, Peter-the-fruit, Chris Wilson (with Sam), Lyn Evans (with Iestyn), John Collyer, Dave Roberts (far better known as Dave-the-train) and Kerry Nicholas's parents, Clive and Sue.

The Holyhead officials made sure that their guests were comfortable and had welcome hot drinks on arrival. Both chairman Alan Hinchliffe and secretary Richard Parry had gone out of their way before and during the afternoon to ensure that the day ran smoothly for the visitors from the other end of the country.

When I arrived there was snow on the peaks of the nearby mountains. At the start of the match mist had descended and at half-time the horizontal rain and howling wind were coming in from the west. Thank goodness I was under shelter in the pressbox with Gareth.

Although Carmarthen won the game 2-1 to extend their unbeaten run to seven matches, and ease into the last sixteen of the Welsh Cup, the Cymru Alliance side put up a spirited fight. Liam Thomas scored early on; Holyhead replied in first-half added time, with the Old Gold winner finally arriving a minute from time when Thomas scored his second of the day. The appreciative crowd (the highest at any ground for today's Third Round fixtures) gave their players a deserved round of applause for an excellent display against higher league opposition.

Afterwards Aize was full of praise for his makeshift back four. "We went into the game without both of our first choice centre-backs and we had to field seventeen year old youth team player Iestyn Evans for his Welsh Cup debut. He had a baptism of fire but came through it."

Mark was now, as usual, getting into his stride and mentioned five others. "We have young footballers who are in their first full season for the club. Players such as Liam Thomas, Sam Wilson, Casey Thomas, Jonathan Hood and Corey Thomas are still learning the game and adjusting to the standards required from them by the management team to play at this level. They will have benefitted enormously from going to such a difficult place as Holyhead and grinding out a result."

"Our game plan did not work out as I had hoped so I was pleased to see how the players have learnt to keep going, and slowly but surely they turned the game around by sticking to their discipline. Also, I was delighted that Craig Hughes [nicknamed 'Guppy'] played his first full ninety minutes of the season. It has been a frustrating time for him with his injury problems, but having him back is like signing a new player."

After all of the media commitments had been satisfied I was able to relax back in the clubhouse while we waited for the draw for the next round. A 'phone message told us that the Reserves had beaten Bancffosfellen 7-0 in their cup match so two wins in a day was more than acceptable.

Finally the S4/C football show got around to conducting the draw. We were the third ball out of the bag, so at least we had a home tie. Then came the fourth: Bala Town! Aizlewood's face became taut. Ooh, I'm looking forward to this clash already.

The *Sgorio* programme the following Monday night announced that Aize had won the WPL's Manager-of-the-Month Award for November. Experience will normally tell you that this Award has been a kiss-of-death experience for many managers in the past. Anyway, watching the film clips from our match at Holyhead did show one unnerving item: at least five seconds of our manager actually smiling during a game. It was unreal television.

The week prior to the game at Bangor was cold and frosty. Then came the mild air and rain which resulted in waterlogged grounds and the postponement of two matches at which I was going to report. Going west from Chester on the Saturday morning had me somewhat worried as the pulses of very heavy rain were causing surface water flooding on the main trunk road.

However, I need not have worried as the pitch at Nantporth was heavy, but playable. The Menai Strait was calm and inviting with the view through the trees from the pressbox showing some interesting properties on the opposite Anglesey bank. For once I had no shopping list for the nearby Waitrose supermarket so it was soon down to work.

The *Sgorio* camera crew had taken some pre-match shots but wanted to be involved with the Manager-of-the-Month presentation. Robert O'Leary from Corbett Sports had arrived and needed to set up his backdrop so we found a perfect spot in front of the main stand. Then the management team of Aize, Kevin Morris and Neil Smothers (better known as Smudger) took part in the short ceremony and following that the *Sgorio* team did their necessary audio-visual filming of which, alas, most ended up as outtakes.

The back of the visitors' dressing room door had had pages of instructions taped on it by Keiran Davies, the club's coaching analyst. The tactics Aize and Smudger had prepared were so detailed that I became boss-eyed trying to focus on their meaning so I left them to it and wandered off to get some teamsheets. Secretary Gwynfor Jones was in his office so I also took the opportunity of letting him know how much I had enjoyed reading his submission to the Welsh Assembly committee.

Before the start of the game I was talking on *Radio Bangor* when the question was asked as to how many people had made the journey from the Carmarthen area. The answer was ten: four in an official capacity; three of the players' parents and three loyal supporters. Little did they then know what the next ninety minutes would bring.

I had buttered up my radio stations with ".... you never know what the curse of the Manager-of-the-Month Award might bring," without fully realising as to how resilient the players had become. It took just eight minutes for a right wing Nicky Palmer cross to be headed firmly into the net by Craig Hughes. Bangor were rocked on their heels but recovered enough to score twice just before the interval.

For half an hour after the break the Old Gold defence held out. The midfield trio of Palmer, Paul Fowler and Corey Thomas worked tirelessly in breaking up attacking movements all the while knowing that Carl Evans, Tim Hicks, Ian Hillier and Craig Hanford were behind them. Steve Cann made three excellent saves in this period which severely frustrated the Bangor players.

Then came the incident which changed the game. A foul in front of the home dugout saw a few handbags thrown around. Players nearby ran to sort out the fracas while others sprinted half the length of the pitch to get involved. Referee Huw Jones stood back and waited for the players to separate and calm down. He then consulted his assistants at length before issuing red cards to Carmarthen's Hughes and Hanford and Bangor's Liam Brownhill.

So it was now nine men against ten, and not for the first time this season the visitors found themselves facing a numerically superior side. Aizlewood's reaction was to then change to a 3-2-3 formation and three minutes from the end of the match up popped Liam Thomas to head in his seventeenth goal of the season. A 2-2 draw was totally unexpected but very welcome and for the third time in a month Carmarthen had knocked a team from the top of the WPL.

Afterwards all the radio broadcast media wanted to talk to Mark, as well as television for the *Sgorio* programme. It took him thirty-five minutes to get through interviews in both Welsh and English before he even thought of turning to me. "It was a magnificent performance to gain a point at the league leaders," he said. "In terms of spirit, character and a determination to succeed, the players have proved their mettle, sometimes in very difficult circumstances."

He then turned his mind to the number of red cards his team has received so far this season. "I am acutely aware that the disciplinary record must be improved but neither I, the management team or the players are here to win house points. While I am concerned about the impact of suspensions, football is a results business not a performance or popularity contest. I will not be asking the players to change their approach as, out of the red cards we have received, only one has been for dissent."

Then came the finale: "Football is a game played by human beings and is full of emotion and passion, which are the qualities that I look for in any player." As Aize left I could not help but agree with what he had said. The game has changed so much in recent years that to have a team with some old-fashioned feeling instilled into them is somewhat of a rarity.

I went to the match official's changing room to see referee Huw Jones to confirm all of the red and yellow cards. He could not have been more pleasant or co-operative and even corrected an error I had made. I left the room knowing that he now had a pile of paperwork to complete and that my football club were yet again firmly rooted to the bottom of the Fair Play League. Ah, well.

Two days later we had a Management Committee meeting in the clubhouse. Fortunately the Academy match scheduled for the evening had been postponed so we did not have to share the room with any of the player's parents.

The main item on the agenda concerned arrangements for next month's League Cup Final at Newtown. An added consideration was an under-age tournament which came with the Final and the shipping of the players and parents to the venue near to Latham Park. Three coaches had been booked so far and if more supporters indicated they wished to travel then a fourth vehicle had to be on standby.

Usually my ability to be diplomatic is at the lower end of any scale of measurement but after a subject had been raised I had to keep pinching myself to shut up: as did at least two others sitting around the table. When you know that there is a problem in a certain area of the club's organisation (as do quite a few people on the terraces) then you hope that the Director, under whose responsibility the matter lies, will bring it forward. If not, and it's not your responsibility, then be silent and smile sweetly.

At the end of the meeting G.O. whispered that he wanted to see me privately. What had I done wrong? We went to the matchday office where Anthony Parnell and Neil Alexander were already sitting around a table. "Sit down, Chris," said the chairman. Shit: I must be in big trouble.

For once in my life I was wrong. I hadn't offended anyone (well, not this week, anyway). The private meeting concerned a communication G.O. had received from another WPL club asking for permission to talk to one of our star players. The discussion was along the lines of 'do we sell?' or 'do we refuse permission.' Eventually we gave our opinions. The result was to give a refusal. Wheels turned within wheels and the player was offered an extended contract. As G.O. was writing out the details, before the player signed some days later, Aize recommended two additional clauses:

(a) The player would only be allowed to speak to another club if that club was in a higher league; i.e. The Football Conference and above, and

(b) That the financial amount offered met the valuation of the said player by Carmarthen Town Association Football Club.

The player duly signed and that was the end of the matter.

It rained all week and Jonathan Lewis worked hard on the pitch to get it playable. "I spent most of yesterday and today working on it," he told me prior to the Friday night fixture against Port Talbot Town. "In fact," he added, "I don't think in all my ten years as groundsman I have seen it so green in late December." The decision to move the match paid off. Not only in the numbers attending but because had it been played at the usual time the following Saturday afternoon it would have been postponed due to a waterlogged pitch.

Adding to Jonathan's worries that evening was the fact that as soon as the floodlights had been switched on smoke started seeping from the fuse box. There was worry all around but the club's luck held and the match was completed without incident.

Yet again the terraces murmured their approval during the ninety minutes of play at the way Mark Aizlewood and Neil Smothers had been able to galvanise the players into a cohesive group who played some excellent football. Following Jonathan Hood's superbly struck goal after a quarter of an hour's play the Old Gold dominated until the break. Then the visitors really put on the pressure but were held back by the central defence in which Matthew Rees was a massive presence.

Steve Cann, in goal, made some splendid saves. In front of him Ian Hillier, Nicky Palmer and Tim Hicks showed their defensive capabilities, and in front of them the industrious Liam McCreesh and Corey Thomas worked tirelessly in midfield. By the time the final whistle sounded the words 'spirit, character and commitment' had passed my lips a number of times when giving radio reports and updates.

After the game Huw, G.O. and I were in the office filing our various pieces of information to necessary organisations when Aize walked in. "We're fifth in the table," he exclaimed before being interviewed in front of the *Sgorio* cameras.

He knew, as we did, that this time last year the club was a gloomy place. Twelve months later the team found themselves in the top half of the WPL table; in the League Cup final and still participating in the Welsh Cup. But, if nothing else, Mark was a realist. In the *Carmarthen Journal* a few days later he said: "I will be emphasising to the players the importance of retaining standards, as a football season is not a sprint to the line. No prizes can be won until May when we will all be judged: and the league table does not lie at the end of the season."

I get loads of sport related stuff shoved through my office letterbox on most days of the week. Some things are interesting; some fairly boring while others are a complete waste of paper. One of the former is a magazine called *UEFA Direct* which is sent monthly from UEFA's headquarters in Nyon, Switzerland. It is a production printed on expensive glossy paper and my usual interest in it is to find out how many delegates from British football associations travel to Nyon to sit on various committees and what would be the amount of their expenses.

The December issue contained a breakdown of the money paid to the 183 clubs who did not qualify for the group stages of either the Champions or Europa Leagues. Quite amazingly the highest amount of €720,000 went to the champions of Luxembourg, F91 Dudelange, who played in the first and second qualifying rounds of the Champions League before being knocked out in the third, and then losing in the Europa League play-offs.

This set me thinking about Carmarthen Town. What if Aize and Smudger get us into the next season's Europa League? What would be the financial benefit to the club? This year Cefn Druids, Bangor City and Llanelli each got €100,000 for just turning up to be knocked out at the first attempt. Win two further ties and the figure jumps to €300,000. Just think how pleased our Director of Finance would be with that sort of money in the bank.

The Boxing Day match against Llanelli was in doubt until about half an hour before kick-off. The heavens had opened and the ground was saturated. Quite a number of people helped Jonathan in forking the ground which referee Dean John eventually passed as playable.

In the office the 'phone kept ringing and as the appointed duty officer I kept telling callers that the game was on. This meant that even on a foul day the number of spectators who turned up saw us record an above average attendance. Not all of the callers wanted to talk about football. Someone from the Carmarthen Angling Club needed to book a clubhouse room for a monthly meeting; a lady from Kidwelly had some old photographs she wanted to show to a committee member; another thought I was her nephew Bob and only became puzzled when she finally stopped talking and heard my accent; with another asking if I had enjoyed my Christmas lunch before suddenly hanging up. No wonder G.O. looks frazzled after some matches.

Eventually I was able to grab my files and papers to head off around the ground to the multi-media centre. Lyn Evans was already in-situ and we were soon joined by Willy Thomas. Jonathan Lewis finally turned up with his high-visibility waterproof jacket dripping water. He had been at the ground working on the pitch since early morning and the sight of a tin full of my wife's Welsh Cakes soon saw his hunger pangs satisfied.

The game was never going to be a classic on such a heavy ground but both sides put a lot of effort into giving the fans some festive entertainment. With Casey Thomas unable to play due to illness, Carl Evans was selected as an emergency centre-forward and duly scored the only goal of the game. The more elderly of us purred with delight: a 1960s style big burly "Number9" scaring the wits out of smaller defenders. How we cheered at each of his clumsy moves.

Afterwards we gathered in the matchday office. Huw Davies was sending out the day's details to various people as well as updating the club's website; Gwyn Derfel was compiling reports for his WPL website while I was setting out the afternoon's statistics. "I've never seen so many media men," said G.O., which was the signal for *Sgorio's* camera crew to appear to set up for post-match interviews.

Mark Aizlewood arrived in a very good mood. He proceeded to give an interview in Welsh about Carmarthen's tenth successive game without defeat before making a final statement in English. He had been asked why the turnaround in the club's fortunes had happened. "Why?," he said. "Because I'm a fucking genius, that's why." With that he left the room and the laughter behind.

The return match at Stebonheath Park three days later was always going to be a challenge. Five of the team had picked up the vomiting and diarrhoea bug which was laying low a good percentage of the population, with Sam Wilson unable even to travel the short distance to Llanelli. Fitness tests were carried out prior to the start and a makeshift team eventually walked out onto the field.

Llanelli were ready and within ten minutes were two goals to the good. Liam Thomas scored twice in reply but a penalty given away seconds before the break saw the home side gain an interval lead. Llanelli scored again not long after the break and although Aizlewood put on two injured players in Carl Evans and Paul Fowler it made no difference to the score.

Things got worse. Liam McCreesh picked up two yellow cards in four minutes to earn his third suspension of the season and Aize, in protesting too volubly, was sent to the stand for the second time in two months.

Next to me in the pressbox was the referee's assessor, Ray Ellingham. After Ray had made all of his notes regarding both incidents we spoke about the potential number of games McCreesh might miss through suspension. We await the verdict from the FAW in Cardiff.

Some time after the final whistle I was hanging around the player's tunnel waiting to get Aize in front of the cameras. "He's in with the referee," said Llanelli's programme editor Neil Dymock. We waited: it seemed ages before the Carmarthen manager appeared and then he went to be interviewed. I strolled back around the ground towards the clubhouse when Ray caught up with me.

"What happened in there?," I asked, and Ray gave me the gist of what had gone on. It appeared that there was a consensus from the players of both sides that McCreesh had been treated very harshly by referee Richard Harrington but, as two yellow cards had been shown, no appeal was allowable. Aize, on the other hand, had confessed to both encroaching on to the pitch and swearing at the referee.

Later, back in the clubhouse, I conducted a taped interview with Mark. He spoke about the day's defensive problems; looked at the last two league matches before the split; defended McCreesh saying "he won the ball fairly in both tackles" and gave nothing away about any possible new signings once the January transfer window opened.

The players, management team and officials then slowly drifted away. I would not see any of them again in 2012. I sat at the far end of the dining room gabbling into my mobile 'phone dictating copy to a completely unflustered copytaker. I finished, sat back and reflected. It had been a fascinating year both on and off the field. If the club's hierarchy had learnt anything it surely would have been to always appoint a complete professional to manage your team; one who would get the respect of the players and supporters.

Aizlewood had gained that respect through diligence and hard work. Sometimes I felt he was pushing himself too hard but in all of my journalistic years on the football circuit he was by far the most co-operative and considerate of all the managers I have had the fortune, and misfortune, to know. Some fourteen years ago, at a Manchester United press conference, I asked a politically incorrect question and duly received the 'hairdryer' treatment from manager Alex Ferguson. Even with some of his strange habits and idiosyncratic ways that is something Aize would never contemplate.

Manager of the Month Award

CUP SUCCESS AND THE SPLIT

The new year arrived and, with Leon Jeanne having moved to Taff's Well, I was waiting to hear if we had made any bids for players to bolster the squad. It did not take long for G.O. to pass on the news that the management team wanted to sign midfielder Luke Cummings from Bath City and striker Christian Doidge from Barry Town.

I met them at Wednesday training, before they had officially been transferred, and found them both most pleasant people. However, I was distracted from chatting with them by the way Aize was conducting the tactical plans for Saturday's match at Connah's Quay. Another WPL manager had briefed him on the strengths and weaknesses of the North Wales' club's players and this was being drummed into the heads of the Carmarthen team.

My wife and I had made a late decision to travel north on Friday with a stop for a couple of hours in Shrewsbury. I duly found an antique market and was ferreting through piles of old books when she hobbled towards me having fallen awkwardly down some stairs. By the time we arrived at our overnight stay her leg had got worse so she put on an ice-pack and spent the evening on the bedroom sofa.

I went off to watch the Cymru Alliance clash between near neighbours Buckley Town and Flint Town United. It was a superb game of football expertly refereed by Martin Roberts, an official deservedly rising through the ranks rather quickly. The 5-3 scoreline could, in reality, have been anything. The attacking style played by both sides was a joy to behold while each team's woodwork was rattled at regular intervals.

As usual I sat at the back of the stand making notes in my customary way. To my right was a youngish man dressed in a club tracksuit and looking as though he was scouting. Shortly after he had sat down another similar individual joined him and they started talking. Very quickly I realised that the first man was the Connah's Quay manager Mark McGregor and the discussion was about the tactics to be used the next day when Carmarthen Town were to play at the Deeside Stadium.

I started scribbling notes on what was being said when McGregor turned to look at me in a quizzical manner. "You a groundhopper?" he said. I nodded and so, satisfied at my answer, he carried on with his conversation. Eventually his friend went away and at half-time he too disappeared. Immediately I started writing a lengthy text to Aize detailing what I had heard. I think it proved to be useful.

The following morning it became obvious that my wife's plan to go shopping in Chester would have to be cancelled. So after showing her the delights of some of the North Wales coast we arrived at the ground just after the team bus had disgorged its occupants. I went to find physiotherapist Gary Morris to see if he could assess the damage done to her leg. His conclusion was that there was no fracture just ligament damage.

With the assistance of the Connah's Quay secretary Trevor Green we were able to park my car by the side of the running track which surrounded the pitch. However, once certain visiting supporters were made aware that my wife was in the car they came sniffing around to see if, by chance, there was any of her delicious home-made cake available. There was, and soon there were satisfied smiles on a number of faces. I was more than pleased to realise that by default this would be the seventy-seventh ground at which she had watched football. I did wonder if this was a record for a woman living in Carmarthen.

Like all sports stadia the facilities were of a good standard. The changing rooms were modern and convenient, and between them was the secretary's office. I had never really had a chance to talk at length with Trevor Green before and, after a while, when realising we both had certain similar London connections, we were exchanging rumour, scandal and libelous gossip as if it was going out of fashion.

Iestyn Evans Geoff Kellaway Christian Doidge Luke Cummings

The Saturday morning edition of the *Daily Post* had a lengthy preview article on the game. Mark McGregor was quoted as saying: "This is probably the most important match of the season for us. A win today and we will go above Carmarthen, with a game in hand. We can have no bigger incentive than that." When I mentioned this to Aize he replied in a comparable way.

Once referee Huw Jones had started the game it became crystal clear that both sets of players were nervous. The Old Gold gave away a goal after seven minutes when the defence fell for a sucker punch. The same time into the second-half saw the visitors equalise and that it how the score stood at the end. Aize, as always, praised his team for their effort. "When the opposition goalkeeper is man-of-the-match, you know that your team has performed well."

In the eighty-eighth minute Connah's Quay made a substitution. Rhys Healey, making his penultimate appearance for the club before moving to Cardiff City, was replaced by Lee Davey. On his Connah's Quay debut Davey was on the field for five minutes; had three touches of the ball, one of which could have led to a goal scoring opportunity. Little did anyone realise at the time the significance of his appearance.

The build-up to the League Cup final started early in the week. The first thing I needed to know about was attire: do I wander in wearing my usual scruffy football outfit or is it 'Number Ones' as my military relatives used to say. An email to G.O. elicited the reply (copied to all the Directors) gently advising on the desirability of wearing the club tie. This caused my wife to start to ransack the wardrobe to make sure I had all of the necessary accoutrements. "You wear a tie once every six months," she said while moving piles of clothes around. "Where is it?"

*Andrew Thomas and
Jonathan Lewis*

Then came the need to issue a press release which was quickly snapped up by the *South Wales Evening Post* and the *Western Mail*, and later in the week by the *Carmarthen Journal*. After this came a request from Gwyn Derfel for an article for the matchday programme. This was then followed by FAW queries on player photographs while at the same time *Radio Carmarthenshire* and associated stations were trying to organise a broadcast schedule.

On Wednesday Rondo Media wanted to interview Liam Thomas and Iestyn Evans

G.O. with cake

Director of Communications

for a *Sgorio* preview programme to be shown prior to the match. It was filmed upstairs in the clubhouse and, as always, Arwyn Williams oozed professionalism in his organisation of the session. Afterwards I spoke with him about producing documentaries and mentioned that I had made a few for television back in the late-1980s. In those days you could aim to get four minutes worth of final footage from each day in the editing booth. "Nothing's changed," he told me. "Even in 2013 it's still four minutes per day."

Thursday saw Neil Alexander, G.O. and Iestyn travel to Newtown, where the final was to be held, to join a couple of TNS players and Gwyn Derfel for a publicity photo-shoot at a local primary school. The result was a number of syndicated pictures which showed them with an excited group of ankle-biters who were all given free match tickets for their troubles.

Back in my office the 'phones did not seem to stop ringing. Virtually all South Wales newspapers and sports agencies wanted team line-ups, scores, scorers, updates and reports during the day from an hour pre-match until final quotes had been filed, which is normally two hours after the game has finished. Then some asked for 'phone-photos of the winning team being presented with the Cup. If it's Carmarthen then that's all right: if it's TNS we will not have anyone available.

G.O. and Iestyn Evans

When you have been in this business as long as I have (from 1966 with the then broadsheet *Kentish Times*) you get into various ways which come in very useful in times such as these. Quotes from Aize stating: "We have nothing to lose on the day. Saints are expected to beat us comfortably, especially as their players are full-time footballers who can train every day and plan their tactics accordingly," received a wide circulation in South Wales and beyond.

This was just what I wanted. That would keep people's minds focused on 'the poor underdog team who would be taking on the giants.' The day before the big match is an absolutely ideal time in which to pull the rug from underneath your opponents by running an emotional or farewell story. The plan worked to perfection.

At five o'clock on the Friday afternoon I had the four paragraph story ready. The League Cup Final would be thirty-nine year old Julian Alsop's final game after a career which had stretched for twenty-two years and taken in numerous clubs. Not only had he scored the winning goal in a play-off final at Wembley but he also holds the record for the fastest ever hat-trick in senior football.

Within the hour the story had gone viral. Anything concerning TNS appeared to have been wiped clear as the Alsop story dominated the electronic media. The phones rang and radio interviews were carried out. It was all Alsop.

The day of the final arrived and so did the Welsh newspapers, most of which never usually even bother to mention Carmarthen football. Today was different and it seemed to bolster the numbers of 'The Julian Alsop Fan Club' who travelled in their own coach to Newtown for the match.

The morning was cold and on the way to Rhayader there were a few snow flurries but nothing to cause any concern. A late breakfast had been organised at the Strand Bistro with my early arrival causing some disquiet to the Manageress. I asked for access to the area we normally use as I was soon to start a half an hour live radio broadcast. Because the room had not been booked in advance I was told it could not be used but once my producer 'phoned to organise timings she relented and opened up, for the last thing she wanted were loud interviews interrupting the mid-morning refreshments of the town's octogenarians.

As I was starting to speak so Mark Aizlewood, Neil Smothers, Kevin Morris and others arrived. I finished my three pieces before Aize and Smudger took over. This allowed Craig Hughes, who by then had arrived with most of the other players, to film Smothers behind his back and to then download the result on to social networking sites.

The feeling I got from the players was that they were slightly nervous and a bit edgy. Their breakfast food was always the same: beans on toast; scrambled eggs on toast or both, with two having extra toast. Sod the expense: but not really as at training three days earlier chairman Neil Alexander had given kit-man Gareth Davies £150 to cover the cost. We left before the management and players had finished, and immediately ran into two of the coachloads from Carmarthen who were walking to the Bistro for a lunch stop.

On arrival at Latham Park we joined the Rondo Media television crew who were setting up for the day. They had an extra Outside Broadcast (OB) van and what seemed like double the number of technicians and cameramen. I was able to give the producer details of our team which meant that the graphics could be set up early and tested on-screen long before the TNS line-up was passed through.

Once my assistant and I had set up in the pressbox alongside two other radio broadcasters I was able to go into the warmth of the boardroom. The first person I met was the Newtown chairman, Elwyn Preece, who told me the startling news that he was going to step down from his position owing to pressure of work. If he does carry this out it will be a big loss to the club as I have always associated him, and secretary Owen Durbridge, as part and parcel of the game in the town.

Then WPL Secretary Gwyn Derfel arrived and he hardly had time to sip at his cup of tea before the demands of television and the sponsors called him away. He was immediately replaced by the FAW's Head of Competitions Department, Andrew Howard, who soon stopped me worrying. I had been concerned as to who was going to supply match detail and copy to national outlets such as the *Press Association*, *Sky Sports* and *Soccerfile Wales*. He was taking on the task which was a huge relief as we had enough work on our hands.

Then I met Lucy Kelly who had spent ages putting together the matchday programme and printing it in-house. Lucy's title at the FAW is Competitions Officer but I really think that she is the wheel which makes the office turn. A most welcome visitor who joined us as we were talking was former WPL Secretary, John Deakin, now retired and living on the South Wales coast. It was also an opportune moment for me to mention to the FAW's Referees' Manager, Rodger Gifford, about the excellent officiating I had witnessed the previous week at Buckley.

The pre-match events had started earlier in the day with a junior football tournament at the nearby leisure centre. Then came the Newtown Brass Band whose oompah, oompah could be heard quite clearly by the *Radio Carmarthenshire* listeners as I gave a preview story an hour before the start.

I never like going into the dressing room, more so before a game, but had to in G.O's enforced absence to get the teamsheet signed and handed to the referee. The players appeared slightly edgy, as did the management, but nowhere near as uptight as I have witnessed in the past with other teams.

The Carmarthen supporters, who seemed to greatly outnumber the TNS fans, made a huge noise as the teams walked down from the top of the main stand and onto the heavy pitch. There were presentations to be made and the only person I recognised in the official party was the Welsh team manager Chris Coleman. In the pressbox and in the overflow media seating we prepared ourselves. Referee Nick Pratt blew his whistle and the Welsh Premier League Cup Final 2013 was underway.

The *Western Mail*'s match report said: "Carmarthen Town held their nerve in a dramatic penalty shoot-out at Latham Park to land the League Cup for only the second time in their history. It was a deserved, thrilling success against their full-time opponents and emphasised the great strides the club has made under the leadership of Mark Aizlewood and Neil Smothers."

"Veteran Carmarthen midfielder Nicky Palmer, who was voted Man-of-the-Match, was elated with his side's success. "We deserved it because of our work rate," he said. "Everyone had a job of work to do and did it well. Full marks to the coaches who got the tactics spot on. I'm pleased for the club as I've been here a number of years now and I'm chuffed."

"Steve Evans' controversial headed goal in the seventh minute, after Chris Marriott had appeared to foul Palmer, gave fancied TNS an early lead. But, three minutes from the break, a mistake by Chris Seargeant let in Craig Hughes for the equaliser. This lifted the Old Gold for the second half although they did suffer an initial setback."

"Carmarthen goalkeeper Steve Cann seemed frozen to the spot as the talented Sam Finley drove a long range shot past him in the fifty-eighth minute, but Aizlewood's side hit back in style. Two troublesome long throws from Ian Hillier caused chaos in the TNS penalty box and substitute Corey Thomas swooped to drive home two beautifully executed shots to put Carmarthen in front."

"A headed equaliser five minutes from time by Michael Wilde took the tie into extra time. Then came the penalties and it was the men in gold who held their nerve. TNS missed three of their four attempts, with Cann's save from his opposite number Paul Harrison taking the Cup to Richmond Park."

There is such a thing as pressbox etiquette and so, as always, no emotion is ever shown although deep down we can have as much anxiety as anyone else. My charming assistant spent much of the day dictating copy and statistics to the *Mid-Glamorgan Press* and other agencies after which she put on her photographers' bib to record the after-match presentation and celebrations.

Not long after the first TNS goal it became apparent that Paul Fowler was struggling. As Aize said later: "In the twenty-second minute I was faced with a dilemma. Paul was feeling unwell which was clearly due to an illness which had not been evident in the build-up to the game. After a discussion with Neil, we made the change, and put on Corey Thomas as a substitute. This was a risky decision but one which had to be made."

Sitting in the dugout was General Manager, Kevin Morris. The following morning he sent an email to Aize saying: "The decision to bring off Fowls after twenty-two minutes was the bravest decision I have ever seen. To be honest I thought 'you can't do that now. Are you mad!' Obviously not. You are a genius." In an email to me Kevin wrote: "Only he could do that."

As the first-half went through its paces I became more and more aware that the Carmarthen team were following Aize's game plan to the letter. He had sent it to me the previous Tuesday and my feeling, on studying the contents, was that the match would be attritional. It wasn't: that is why he is a coach and I'm in the pressbox.

Before Craig Hughes' equaliser it was becoming clear that the TNS management duo of Carl Darlington and Craig Harrison would need to make tactical changes during the interval. If they did then they were not apparent, for their defence was all at sea for Corey's two goals and subsequent attempts by Hughes (twice), Luke Cummings, Casey Thomas (twice) and substitute Christian Doidge.

After extra-time came the dreaded penalty shoot-out. As the team gathered on the pitch around Aizlewood he gave them but one instruction: "Do not be clever. If you're going to miss then make sure the goalkeeper has to save it."

Carmarthen went first and Tim Hick's shot was saved by Paul Harrison. Then came TNS substitute midfielder Ryan Fraughan who, in trying to be cocky, chipped his effort over the crossbar. Had it been an Old Gold player who had done that then Aize's fury would have been a sight to behold.

Corey Thomas and TNS's Alex Darlington both scored: 1-1. Liam Thomas strode up to fire the ball into the roof of the net. Chris Seargeant then fired over the bar: 2-1. Now the tension was mounting. Craig Hanford left-footed in a third. Steve Cann took over in goal to face his rival custodian. Harrison shot to Cann's left; the ball accurate and well placed. Suddenly a diving figure in light blue pounced; the ball was pushed around the post. Carmarthen Town had won the League Cup.

But there was one thing that the players did not know. The prize money was £10,000 for the winners and £3,000 for the losers. Those penalty kicks had been worth £7,000.

Craig Hughes & Kevin Morris

Mark Aizlewood

Gary Morris

Neil Smothers & Paul Fowler

Tim Hicks

Liam Thomas & Nicky Palmer

Talking tactics

Rob Thomas

Guppy on the prowl

Guppy supervising

Who else?

Arriving late

The Word Cup

Before kick-off

Craig Hughes' goal

Corey's first goal

The defence at work

Carmarthen's third goal

The tension mounts

Saved!

The rush

My hero!

Success

Exaltation

Celebration

Joy

Winners!

Going to collect the Cup

After the Presentation

"I love you all!"

Casey & Corey

With Sgorio

Mark Aizlewood

95

*Mike Davies with
Nicky Palmer*

Aize with the Cup

Triumphant Supporters

Rhys Felton with Julian Alsop

Rhys and Liam

Our hero

I love you Guppy

Chris Coleman and Jack Hannington

With BBC Radio Cymru

Presentation to Gareth Davies

Luke Cummings

The Cup

The presentations were made on the first-floor balcony of the Newtown clubhouse. Matthew Rees collected the cup and the team were showered with bubbly fizz. It was as if the living nightmare of twelve months earlier had never existed. Nicky Palmer was interviewed for television; Aize by *BBC Radio Cymru*. We were still going strong with radio reports and copy to Agencies.

It had been a lovely day, especially for the little things which stuck in the memory. For example, during the break before the start of extra-time Gwyn Derfel had suddenly arrived in the media area with cups of hot drinks. That was the journalist coming out in him for he knew that on a freezing cold day we could not move because of our continual work. His understanding was very much appreciated.

Then, afterwards in the bar, appeared the tall figure of Julian Alsop who seemed rather embarrassed by the loud cheer given to him. A glass of beer was put into his hands at the same time his hero-worshipping fan club burst through the door chanting his name. After a moment they saw his drink and started to chant: "Down in one; down in one; down in one," to which their hero obliged to raised cheers from the whole room.

Outside Aize was coming to grips with it all. He did not let the immediate success go to his head and was already analysing some of the mistakes made by his players. But there was one little thing which you could see pleased him deep down. "Do you know," he told our little group, "that because of the extra-time and penalties our live television broadcast over-ran and *S4/C* actually cancelled showing the rugby." For that to happen in Wales really is a rarity.

The Cup was entrusted to Michelle Hopkins who travelled back to Carmarthen on the coach along with the Alsop fan club. "They were a bit boozy," she said, "and so I wouldn't even let them touch it." On arrival back at Richmond Park the trophy was safely placed in a locked cupboard for the rest of the weekend.

The next morning Aize was ready with his thoughts for me to tidy up and send off to the newspapers which cover South Wales and beyond. I really did not need to do much as his opening line was: "Wonderful. Fantastic. Brilliant. Unbelievable." It needed no changing as it just summed up the day.

"Those would be my four adjectives to describe the performance of the players," he said. "I'm sure that the Old Gold supporters, who made up the bulk of the crowd at Latham Park, would have many other superlatives to describe our amazing win. Along with Neil we work constantly with the players but even now we can still be surprised by the resilience, character and levels of fitness they can achieve. Things like dogged determination and spirit are innate: you are unable to train these into players. But, if you add things such as a game plan, fitness, organisation and tactics, which you train into them, you may be surprised as to how far you can go."

On Monday morning Rondo Media filmed the introduction of the evening's *Sgorio* programme from both upstairs in the clubhouse and outside by the club sign which is attached to the wall. Then it was a matter of finding out where in the country Aize might possibly be found (Manchester, as it turned out) as *BBC Radio Wales* wanted him for the early evening sports show.

But as is the way of the world today nothing passes by the monster which is social media. There were two comments on Twitter. The first from Mike Jones, the General Manager of Rhyl Football Club who commented: "Nice to see the trophy going to a Welsh club in Wales." An immediate retort came back from a TNS user, who added sarcastically: "It was nice to see they did it without using drugs or money they did not have. Well done Old Gold." Really, children. Do behave.

Aize had telephoned on the Tuesday afternoon to let me in on a secret. "The Cup win is in the record books now," he said, "and no one can take that away from me. I've got a medal and quite honestly, Chris, I'll probably put it in a drawer and forget about it. But Gareth [Davies] does so much unpaid work for the club as our kit-man I really feel that he deserves it much more than me. So what I intend to do at training tomorrow is to present it to him. It's something I want to do."

Dave Roberts

Just before training started the following evening Aize called Gareth to one side and told him what he wanted to do. Poor Gareth was completely taken aback and despite his protestations he finally accepted the medal, and then smiled for the cameraman who just happened to have followed him.

The first substantial snowfall of the year gripped the eastern part of South Wales on the third Friday of January. The weather forecasters had indicated a 'red alert' for the hills and valleys while in Carmarthen we had a light dusting. I had a number of emails during the day from contacts all over England who thought the snow drifts had reached previously unheard of heights. I could only reply:

Carmarthen : Beautiful one day; Perfect the next.

The scheduled match against Newtown was to be the final fixture of the first part of the league season. Afterwards there would be a league of the top six teams with European qualification as the main aim. For the bottom six it would be to strive to avoid relegation.

The top five positions had been decided following the completion of twenty-one matches. Of the remaining seven it was possible that any one of six teams could take that last spot. In sixth position were Connah's Quay who led Carmarthen by a single goal difference but with more goals scored. In reality it was between them and us.

Friday morning brought the news that the Maes Tegid pitch in Bala was covered in snow and unplayable. This meant that their home match with Connah's Quay was postponed. Immediately *S4/C* changed their live match schedule to Richmond Park where there were no concerns about the playing surface. However, what they had not foreseen was the fact that the Newtown team might not travel to Carmarthen.

Having initially booked a coach, then cancelled it, the Newtown hierarchy made the decision to let the players make their own way south. However, as many of them, as well as the coaching staff, lived around Liverpool, Chester and the West Midlands they were reluctant to go anywhere where there had been a forecast

Paul Ashley-Jones

of ice on the roads on the way home. The decision not to play the game was conveyed to the FAW on the Friday afternoon but not to Carmarthen until early on Saturday morning.

The day was a disaster for the Old Gold: sponsors had to be informed and, where appropriate, monies refunded. Food brought in for the lunches and for the players' after-match meals were now surplus to requirements, as were the provisions purchased by the ladies who run the tea-hut. The matchday programmes had been printed and would now need changing for the rearranged date. But what was worse was the fact that the four figure television broadcast fee had been lost.

The following week saw little improvement in the weather. Training was cancelled as even Aize was snowed in. Smudger might just have made it albeit with a struggle while a number of the players had no chance due to the motorway being closed.

I suppose I can get a little tetchy at times, especially when someone starts interfering with the media work I carry out for the club. By lunchtime on Thursday I was ready to throttle a certain individual who had gone a long way to stuffing up my burgeoning relationship with *BBC Radio Wales*. He had not only misrepresented himself to the Corporation but had given them assurances, on behalf of the club, which just could not be kept. The problems he had caused took the rest of the day to unwind and not even then to my total satisfaction.

The last thing I needed prior to the Welsh Cup match against Bala Town was a communications failure. As I passed Aize he said: "I've tried to phone you but there is never an answer." I thought it a bit odd and mentioned it to G.O. who then said the same. A few minutes later came a message that *Radio Carmarthenshire* could not get hold of me. Did I have a problem?

I did. My phone had 'crashed.' A panic call to my wife and a few minutes later she was by my side soothing my fevered brow and swapping mobile phones. An hour and a half later she returned with the news that I now had a new instrument. What was wrong with the old one? It was brand new in 1999? This explanation suddenly caused those around the media centre to burst out laughing. I am not a Luddite.

The travelling fans from Bala told of an initially hazardous journey earlier in the day with ice on the roads until they got to the coast. There must have been at least forty of them and they, like us, experienced a cup match full of twists and turns.

On a heavy pitch, made even worse by a mid-match downpour, Carmarthen should have been three goals to the good before Liam Thomas scored four minutes before the interval. Bala were poor and nothing like the aggressive team we had met twice in the league. The improvement only came fifteen minutes from normal time when they went into an attacking mode. A minute from the end they equalised.

Extra-time loomed; but only for a minute as Liam Thomas found the net once again. The relief lasted for a fraction over two hundred seconds as, just before the end of time added on, Bala equalised again. A further twelve minutes and 'Guppy' had slammed the ball into Bala's net for the final goal of the day.

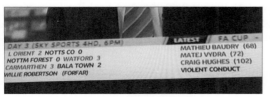

On his way home later in the evening he sent me an email which read: "A great win. I'm now completely shattered. Bed early." I don't think he will be the only exhausted player to express such feelings.

I knew that Kevin Morris had been in contact with a number of players from other clubs to see if they would like to come and play for Carmarthen. There were the usual excuses of money and distance for some refusals but others were just plain mind-numbing. Anyway, the good news was that striker Geoff Kellaway put pen to paper on Monday afternoon.

John Beeden

Geoff had spent a number of seasons with Aberystwyth Town before trying his luck in Australia. He then played in the Victorian State League before moving up to the national A-League. On his return he went back to Park Avenue before moving to Llanelli in the close season. Aize told me: "He will be in the squad for the Newtown game but, please Chris, when you do your press release to the newspapers do emphasise the hard work which Kevin put in to make this transfer possible."

Later in the day came minutes of a WPL meeting and with it an attachment. It was from Gwyn Derfel and was a report of a meeting he had attended in Rome with regard to betting on games and match fixing. It had been organised by INTERPOL and also present were the hierarchy of FIFA and UEFA and representatives from major bookmakers.

I found it a fascinating document. Jerome Valcke, secretary-general of FIFA had said: "Irregular betting and match fixing are considered as the biggest threat to the beautiful game and we need to get rid of these cancers." He added: "FIFA have recently contributed £20 million to INTERPOL for them to investigate and stop these practices. This money will not be solely concentrated on the so-called 'bigger' nations. We have found many cases in Asia and Africa as well as European countries such as Greece, Switzerland, Finland, Macedonia, Germany and Hungary."

Gwyn put an appendix to this report by noting the FAW rules which cover betting. Although my knowledge of the law in this area is poor I did wonder if these rules had ever been tested in court. It seemed to my reading of them that any 'Rumpole' could have torn them to shreds.

But what was of interest was his final statement. "The WPL has informed the Gambling Commission of the details of every player and official involved in the league, who will act swiftly and decisively upon receipt of any information or proof regarding betting on any WPL matches."

Sean Cresser

The build up to the rearranged Newtown game started early in the week when the *South Wales Evening Post* ran Aize's Bala match quotes alongside a forthcoming preview. Then the *Carmarthen Journal* mentioned it followed by *BBC Radio Wales* and the North Wales editions of the *Daily Post*.

Training for the match was interrupted by the fact that the players first had to attend Richmond Park for medical checks. This is a UEFA requirement for our licence applications and meant that when I rolled into the Barn there was only Aize, Paul Fowler and Jonathan Hood present.

After listening to some wonderfully scandalous gossip, none of which I would dare repeat here, Paul asked Aize who had been the best person he had ever played against. The reply was immediate: "No question about it: Ruud Gullit was superb. He knocked me all over the place. You don't realise how tall he is until you stand next to him. He crucified me on the pitch. When the board went up calling him off the pitch I was relieved until I saw who was his substitute: Marco van Basten!"

Chairman, Neil Alexander, wanted to use the match to try and attract more youngsters to Richmond Park. Publicity was thin on the ground as there was a seeming general reluctance by media outlets to do anything more than to make a reference to the fact that the game had a late afternoon kick-off. When talking to the manager of *Radio Pembrokeshire* about the possibility of a mention in their community 'What's On' slot I was taken aback to be told that as we were a profit making body we should pay for any publicity. As you can imagine, the chairman was not amused.

The day before the match interest perked up with Aize giving a lengthy interview to *BBC Radio Wales* who subsequently told me that they would be sending a commentator to give live up-dates. Then *BBC Radio Cymru* decided to broadcast most of the game live which shows how far the club has risen in esteem within sporting circles. Soon newspapers in other parts of Wales started 'phoning with requests for news and background information. It was all a bit surreal.

Had I known in advance what the first Saturday in February held for many of us, I might well have stayed in bed all day with the blankets over my head protecting me from reality. It was a day of pure drama. Fortunately, over the years, my journalistic training and experience has taught me to snap into a high-octane mode to deal with such events.

All seemed so calm three hours before the start. The usual greetings of "what type of cake has your wife made today," came from those whose waistlines did not really need hunks of chocolate cream sponge to savour and enjoy. In the matchday office Gwyn Derfel had already arrived and set up while I started to prepare the paperwork necessary for the day. Fortunately I had pre-recorded a fairly lengthy preview story for *Radio Carmarthenshire* from my office earlier in the day.

The late afternoon start for all games in the WPL had been at the request

| Jan Payne | Cheryl Jenkins | Wendy Davies | Diane Davies |

of the league's television broadcasting partner *S4/C* who, along with Rondo Media, had previously scheduled an international rugby union match for earlier in the day. As kick-off time drew near news filtered through regarding the Reserve team's 7-2 victory away at Swiss Valley with Nicky Thomas scoring four times. Because of the weather it had been their first league game since the end of October.

The few players I met before the start appeared to be very relaxed about the day. They knew that they had to win by three clear goals to possibly pip Connah's Quay to the coveted sixth position in the league table before it was split into two phases. The top six would play each other for the right to participate in European competition next season, while the bottom six would try to fight off relegation.

Both Connah's Quay and Carmarthen started the day on twenty-seven points from twenty-one matches, with the former having a goal difference advantage of one but also having scored eighteen times more. It was as close as that.

Once referee Kevin Morgan had got our game underway news came through that Connah's Quay's opponents Bala Town already had had a man sent off. That set off the groans around the media centre. Then Newtown scored after a quarter of an hour and until half-time the Old Gold just didn't fire. Aizlewood said later: "That was probably the worst forty-five minutes we have served up in a long time. It meant that Neil and I had to work hard to rectify some tactical and other issues."

By now Connah's Quay were three goals up. None of the Carmarthen players knew this as they took to the field for the final forty-five minutes of the regular season. New man, Geoff Kellaway, had already hit a post but after ten minutes scored with a shot which went under Newtown 'keeper Dave Roberts. It took the visitors a further eleven minutes to take the lead again.

It was then that Aize made his third and final substitution taking off defender Ian Hillier and bringing on Christian Doidge, a move which soon paid dividends. Meanwhile Kellaway had thundered a shot against the crossbar. Two minutes later Steve Cann launched a long goal-kick which Doidge, with virtually his first touch of the ball, nodded on to Kellaway. He weaved through the Newtown defence and fired in from the edge of the area: 2-2 with eighteen minutes left on the referee's watch. By then Connah's Quay were leading 5-1.

Four minutes later, with the visiting defence in complete panic, Corey Thomas delivered a superb long cross into the goalmouth where Doidge outjumped the surrounding defenders to nod the ball into the roof of the next for his first goal for the club. Now it was 3-2 at Richmond Park, but 6-1 at Bala.

With one minute of normal time left to play Liam Thomas broke through the

Mike Davies

tiring defence. His shot was blocked but he ran back to collect the ball before sliding it across the face of the goal for Doidge to stab home. The final whistle soon sounded: Carmarthen had won 4-2 but the news from Maes Tegid was that Connah's Quay had won 6-3, so heading us in the final league table by just a two goal difference.

We finished the game just as I was going live on the six o'clock news bulletin. This meant that, unusually, I was back in the matchday office very quickly. As I walked in a flustered looking Gwyn Derfel was just rushing out. He pointed to a pile of papers, which had the words: 'Welsh Premier League Statement Regarding Connah's Quay,' as a heading. "Hello. This looks good," I said to no one in particular and then read the following as Gwyn was being interviewed by Mike Davies for the *Sgorio* programme:

"Connah's Quay has been found guilty by a Football Association of Wales Disciplinary Panel of fielding an ineligible player. The Panel decided to deduct the club one WPL point and fine them £250 for fielding Lee Davey as a late substitute in the league match against Carmarthen Town on 5th January 2013."

It continued, "Davey had previously played for Colwyn Bay and Conwy Borough during the present season and, while he was entitled to register for Connah's Quay, participating for three teams in one season is not permitted. Connah's Quay has seven business days in which to appeal this decision. The club is perfectly within its rights to appeal. The WPL is aware that this may impact on the beginning of the second phase of the WPL."

I walked past Gwyn and Mike as I went to the changing room. The first person I saw was Smudger who said he had heard a rumour so I showed him the press release. It didn't sink in at first what the consequences were until other players read it and shouted out to the others in the shower. All of a sudden I was surrounded by naked men, some tattooed but all dripping water. It was Guppy who first asked the question as to why the information had not been released earlier.

It was a good point but later Gwyn Derfel explained that the decision had been made in order not to interrupt the final round of fixtures. His view was valid for had either Connah's Quay or Carmarthen lost or drawn their games then the whole exercise would have been academic.

As was subsequently revealed, the FAW became aware of the matter about Davey nine days after the event on Monday 14 January. I can only assume that this became known when the players' appearances were being noted from the clubs' new electronic teamsheets which have to be submitted to the league. The WPL then launched an internal investigation and as Gwyn said later: "It took us about two minutes to find that Davey had played for three clubs and about three more minutes to read the match reports which noted his appearances. It was that easy."

Whereas Connah's Quay secretary Trevor Green argued in reply that he had only checked the FAW's 'My Club' database which had a gap in Davey's registration. As Green said: "I thus assumed that he was not in breach of the rule which prevents a player from appearing for more than two clubs in one season."

Later in the day the FAW sent an email to the club, followed by the statutory letter, advising them not to play Davey again and, eight days later, issued a charge against Connah's Quay in accordance with the FAW rules (Rule 43.1.2 if you really want to know).

The club had seven business days to respond stipulating whether they admitted or denied the charge, and Connah's Quay replied on 31 January denying the charge but waiving their right to a private hearing before a Disciplinary Panel. The Panel met the following afternoon and, in the words of the FAW, "in order for the matter to be considered quickly and before knowing the outcome of the Phase One fixtures."

Later that afternoon the decision, and the Panel's grounds for that decision, were communicated to Trevor Green and to the WPL. In its conclusion the FAW stated: "The Panel accept the club's mitigating circumstances concerning the points raised about the 'My Club' database. However, the Panel stressed that the database only provides assistance to clubs but does not fall under the remit of FAW Rules and can only be used as a guide."

As you can imagine the emotional response from Connah's Quay was to argue their corner and to point out the perceived injustice of the Panel's conclusion. Trevor Green's initial reaction was to issue a statement which said: "We apologise for any disruption which might occur to our colleagues as we take our right to appeal. We are innocent of the charge brought against us

by the FAW as both prosecution and jury. We are taking this fight forward and hope you will appreciate why. We will avail of our right to appeal until no appeal process is left open to us. Unfortunately, this may take some time."

The immediate repercussion was the postponement of our next match, which would have been the first of the new phase of the season. Almost without exception it was stated that we were going to North Wales to play Airbus Broughton with the game already rearranged for Easter Monday. No one considered that, should Connah's Quay's appeal succeed, we might be in the bottom group of six with a home fixture against Aberystwyth Town.

The thought of any prolonged appeal sent shudders through the Old Gold's management team. It was going to be bad enough having a free week as Aize and Smudger had built up the team's momentum but the thought of the next match being the Welsh Cup tie against Prestatyn Town in early March was too awful to contemplate.

Behind the scenes things started to move. There were a number of emotional emails winging their way around cyberspace once the full implication of Connah's Quay's threat to appeal and, if necessary, to appeal again sunk in. The final place for any appeal process was the Court of Arbitration for Sport based in Lausanne who, knowing the speed at which they work, would probably be able to decide on the matter by mid-summer. Where would that leave the league programme?

The Directors of Carmarthen Town met the following Tuesday evening and decided not to get involved in anything concerning the whole disciplinary matter. They issued a statement clearly stating their support for both the FAW and WPL, and accepting any further decision whenever it might be made.

Training took place in The Barn the following evening. Aize addressed the players in order to allay any of their fears. He also indicated that there might be a number of behind-closed-doors games arranged to keep them match fit should the appeals process drag on. If the enforced break had any advantage it gave a number of the squad time to recover from injury.

At the end of the first week in February came some good news. Liam Thomas had been chosen as the 'WPL Player of the Month' an award which found considerable favour with his team-mates. In the way of today's social media, and its instantaneous showing of opinion, the congratulations poured in. The citation read: 'Liam Thomas has created a big impression at Carmarthen Town this season. The midfielder caught the eye once again and scored two league goals during January: a month which saw the Old Gold capture the League Cup by beating TNS on penalties.'

Liam Thomas with Gwyn Derfel

Later on the Friday afternoon Connah's Quay announced that they were going to appeal against the FAW Panel's decision.

The five reasons given were obviously drafted by a legal eagle (with little understanding of the mores of football) for they were so nit-pickingly and excruciatingly technical that it made me wonder how many solicitors would be needed by the FAW to guide them through the case.

The next day, instead of going north to Airbus, I found myself at Stebonheath Park where Llanelli were playing Afan Lido. I had been asked to broadcast at regular intervals which gave me time to talk to a number of football officials. One of them suggested that the matter would be resolved in days with behind-the-scenes trade offs settling the matter. I wonder if he will be right?

However, the weekend did have some Carmarthen football. The reserves won their Challenge Cup quarter-final match 2-1 against Swiss Valley with Ian Barrett and Dan Ramsey finding the net. The Academy team had a long haul north to play Flint Town United in the FAW Youth Cup and put on an excellent display to run out 4-2 winners. Goals from Mitchell Escott-Sloan, Sean Bergiers, Iestyn Evans and a Sam Wilson penalty saw them through to the semi-finals.

The settlement of the Connah's Quay issue came, as expected, on Wednesday afternoon. It was announced just too late for us to put into place anything for the scheduled home match against The New Saints but at least the rest of the fixture list could now be released.

It was crystal clear to anyone with a scintilla of knowledge of the way football authorities work that a case of the 'we won't do this to you if you don't do this to us' syndrome had been activated and found to be working in fine order.

The official press release read: 'Connah's Quay have advised the FAW this afternoon (13 February 2013) that the club are withdrawing their appeal against the one WPL point deduction, fine and costs order imposed by the FAW Disciplinary Panel for fielding an ineligible player.'

The statement added: 'Clubs are reminded of their responsibility to undertake stringent checks when registering players. The FAW My Club portal [computer link] does not provide information on whether a player has participated in matches as many leagues are either under area association control or under the jurisdiction of another national association such as the Football Association in England.'

This second paragraph raises more questions than before. How can a governing body admit that they do not have full control over players within their province? To my mind this confession shows the urgent need for FAW staff to undertake a basic administrative shake-up instead of occupying their time on promoting politically correct concepts for the benefit of cheap media coverage and to pacify the chattering classes. An air of amateurishness is blowing around the Welsh football world.

Training that night seemed to be far more intense than usual now that the league problem had been resolved. The players had expressed their pleasure at being placed in the league's top six group judging by their comments on social networking sites. Aize told them about a friendly match which had been arranged at Taff's Well in order to keep them match fit. He did not mention it, but the slap on the wrist he had received from the FAW for being sent from the field at Llanelli must have been a relief.

Bernie Davies

Alan Latham

Paul Evans

Clive Thomas

Alun Williams

Alan Dodd

Antony Powell

Lyn Evans,
Peter (the-fruit) Williams
and
David (Dai Bala) Hughes

THE CHAMPIONSHIP CONFERENCE

The only match involving a Carmarthen Town team, on the third Saturday of February, saw the reserves in action at Whitland. They won 4-0 so extending their lead at the top of the table. "I want to get promotion," said Steve 'Gas' later, "and the fact that eight of our remaining ten games are at home should give us an advantage."

The Academy players were full of anticipation when I saw them two days later prior to their league game against Haverfordwest County. The Welsh Youth Cup semi-final draw had seen them paired with Swansea City in a match which many had hoped would have been the final. The venue was agreed as Stebonheath Park with the Swansea Academy Director, Tony Pennock, asking for a midweek date instead of the usual Sunday playing day.

With a first-team playing squad of twenty-one, Aize was acutely aware that some of the players would probably be left sitting on the bench for most of the rest of the season. So it was little surprise when the news came through that both Sam Wilson and Iestyn Evans were going to sign loan forms enabling them to play for Llanelli. However, the reality was that with their selection for various Welsh schools and under-age sides the actual Play-off Conference matches in which they would participate would be fairly few.

With the UEFA Women's Under-19 Championship to be held in West Wales during the second part of August there are regular inspections of the grounds to be used. We will be hosting five games at Richmond Park and as I am going to be involved on the media side of things G.O. invited me to the latest meeting. The two inspecting visitors were Yolande Seewer from UEFA and Ceri Stennett of the FAW.

They were most impressed at the progress of the building work on the new changing room facility which will also include a fully functional communications office and refreshment area (and an additional twenty-eight keys, according to Jonathan Lewis). Add to this the promise of a levelled and newly laid pitch in the close season and the advantages of staging the tournament become loud and clear.

Driving along the motorway to Cardiff during the rush hour is not something I would wish to do every day. Flashing signs indicated lengthy queues towards Newport but fortunately the turn for Taff's Well was before any of the problems.

Then it was through the Moy Road Industrial Estate, where Kevin Morris (our own Abramovitch, according to Aize) has his luxurious offices, and on into the Parish Road ground.

As always at Taff's Well Football Club the first person I met was secretary Norma Samuel. She had everything organised for the evening, even down to the after-match pizza about which I had been very complimentary on our previous visit last August.

In an attendance of twenty for the evening's entertainment, eight had travelled east. Clive and Sue Nicholas with entourage sat in the stand along with John Collyer and myself, with Howard Williams and Peter (the-fruit) Williams being kit-men for the night in the absence of Gareth Davies.

To balance the sides we loaned Taff's three of our squad, all of whom either scored or smacked the ball against the woodwork. The result was 3-3 with Liam Thomas scoring twice and Paul Fowler striking a superb twenty-five yard effort. But it was the injuries which caused me most concern, especially the one to Carl Evans' knee, but Aize said there was nothing to worry about. Even so, I later found out that Jonathan Hood (who was not an initial injury worry) had spent the night in hospital at Bridgend suffering from chest pains.

Two days later I received an email from G.O. asking if I could take a number of photographs after the Academy match against Pontardawe Town. He wanted snaps of some of the players with Martin Evans, the Welsh Schools' Football Association's Under-18 manager. The evening was bitterly cold so I joined Andrew Thomas by the upstairs clubhouse windows near to which I could put a table for all the papers needed for the evening.

Iestyn Evans, Sam Wilson, Martin Evans and Dafydd Jones

The Pontardawe followers (mainly parents) were a cheerful crowd and the social evening passed all too soon, even while the teams on the field were battling out a 1-1 draw. After the photoshoot I went back into the warmth to spend a pleasant hour with Academy player Callum Jackson's mother Alyth.

Then Mark Hannington (the club's chef and third choice goalkeeper) presented me with supper: sometimes it is very difficult to leave Richmond Park.

The day before we resumed hostilities in the WPL came two pieces of news. Sam and Iestyn had decided not to go on loan to Llanelli, mainly because of their representative commitments, while Jonathan Hood had made the decision to accept a transfer to Caerau, a club who play in Welsh League Division Two. Hood had joined Carmarthen in January 2012 and in his time with us he had been dogged by injury. Aize thought it best to let him go which would, in all probability, extend his football career.

Mark Hannington

The morning of the Bangor game was cold with the temperature hardly rising above freezing point. I wandered into the clubhouse at lunchtime to find Aize already in residence and, having worked out his team formation, he gave me the details which meant that I could organise my radio preview piece with plenty of time before the broadcast.

The players came strolling in one by one with the main point of discussion being the age and state of the car Geoff Kellaway was driving. His protestations of it being his wife's vehicle made the ribald comments even more exaggerated.

Huw Davies was already in residence in the matchday office so once I had given him the team for the website I could turn to taking even more photographs. Steve Cann was going to sign an extended contract so it was the usual group snaps with manager and coach, then with the chairman. I'll give Huw his due; the photos were on the website and social media pages in a very quick time.

As the match was about to start some of our usual group turned up but others were missing. It was just Jonathan, Willy, Ifor and myself with all of us wondering why the visit of a quality team such as Bangor could not draw the crowds. Maybe they knew something more than we did for the game was attritional to say the least.

Bangor took the lead after eleven minutes and then packed their defence. As time wore on so my sometimes ludicrous statistics came to the fore: we had not yet had a corner and as the visitor's total rose so the suspense grew. Suddenly my lead comment for the after-match broadcast was going to be: "This has been Carmarthen's first cornerless match since August 2005 ...."

Aize, Steve Cann and Smudger

Then Sod's Law struck. In the third minute of added time we won our only corner of the game. The mirth and merriment which erupted from our group even distracted a couple of the players who looked at us in a puzzled way.

After the game Aize, as usual, put it bluntly. "My team were just not match fit. In no way does my disappointment about the defeat involve the players. It was our first competitive match for three weeks and it looked it. We were nowhere near to the team we were in our last match against Newtown. We had completely lost the momentum we had built up and which we were originally going to take into the second phase of the league season."

"I do not wish to take anything away from a Bangor side who did a professional job, but it was not Bangor that beat us. It was the situation my players found themselves in. Along with Neil, I tried everything possible to keep the players 'match-fit' but the term explains itself and means you can only do this by playing matches."

"The very fact we only lost by the odd goal, and possibly even deserved a draw, is testimony to the players' attitude and character. They were obviously not at their best but kept going throughout the ninety minutes. This is a quality we will need in abundance between now and the middle of May."

"We now have eighteen first-team players [not including Sam and Iestyn on national duty] for the rest of the campaign. Neil and I will be constantly rotating team selection. This is to ensure that every player will be totally match fit for the season's latter stages."

Later on, after getting news of the Reserve team's 3-1 win at Penyfan, I happened to glance at the matchday programme. In it was an article written by Jeff Thomas in his role as the club's Business Director. He said: "You will have noted the absence of match sponsors for today's game. This is indeed a rare event other than during the month of August when there is a complete lack of interest [due to the holiday season]."

Jeff continued: "However, one debate continues to form part of our discussions and that is of the WPL split; dividing the top and bottom six clubs in mid-January. We are all aware of the recent delay due to an FAW disciplinary matter which ended with us being elevated to the WPL top group and today sees our deferred start to Phase Two of the season."

Jeff Thomas

"The wait and uncertainty will cost our club many thousands of pounds. This will be further compounded by us having to play a rescheduled midweek match against The New Saints which is always a plum fixture in attracting Saturday sponsors. I must also add that I have not witnessed the usual gusto by sponsors in wishing to attend games following the introduction of the current league system. They, like spectators, are voting with their feet."

Jeff's feelings are virtually universal within the Welsh football community except, that is, for a small coterie based around a boardroom table in an office near to Cardiff docks.

Saturday dawned and with it a day which felt as if spring had at last come around. I arrived at the ground for the Welsh Cup quarter final match against Prestatyn Town about three hours before kick-off to find Aize conducting a quiz competition with most of the team. I stood and watched, realising very quickly that I was an old fogey compared to the players. Many football questions which Aize asked were about events which took place before they were born. Some of the looks of complete bemusement were better than thousands of words.

However, it was a wonderful move in order to try and tighten even further the spirit within the team. Their whoops and shouting showed a definite competitive nature which, obviously, the management team wanted to transfer to the pitch itself. After the successful group had collected their winnings and gone off to lunch I wandered downstairs to chat with Gwyn Derfel who

Chris Wilson

had come to Richmond Park to officially present Liam Thomas with his Player-of-the-Month cheque.

I had copied Gwyn in on an email I had circulated a couple of days earlier and we spent a while talking about it. What I had done was to go through the FAW records to find out details of the 292 players who had played in the WPL (formerly the League of Wales) for Carmarthen Town. My idea was to give each player an individual number as is done in international cricket and some representative rugby.

He felt that the idea had considerable merit but wondered if the research work would be too much for some of the other clubs who might also wish to take on the idea. Alas, I had to agree. However, the concept of putting our players' numbers on the matchday shirts was given the green light so long as it was agreed by club officials.

For our current players their individual numbers in order of appearance for the Old Gold are: Tim Hicks 111; Neil Smothers 183; Craig Hughes 189; Paul Fowler 203; Nicky Palmer 221; Craig Hanford 232; Corey Thomas 262; Steve Cann 279; Ian Hillier 280; Carl Evans 282; Matthew Rees 283; Liam Thomas 285; Casey Thomas 286; Kerry Nicholas 287; Liam McCreesh 288; Luke Cummings 290; Christian Doidge 291; Geoff Kellaway 292.

Mark Aizlewood then joined us and as it was obvious he wanted to talk to Gwyn I wandered off. Even from some yards away I could hear Mark explaining that the enforced break, due to the Connah's Quay situation, had made the team lose their impetus and thrust. While the WPL secretary was sympathetic and understood Aize's view I could quite understand that there was little more he could have done in the circumstances.

In the clubhouse I bumped into the Prestatyn chairman Phil Merrick and secretary Gareth Owens. Whenever Phil and I are together we always seem to talk about our books. Phil's latest, *Bleed White*, about the last ten years behind the scenes at Leeds United, seems to be selling quite well and the reviews have also been favourable.

Pleasant as their company may have been, quite the opposite had to be said for the accompanying Prestatyn 'fans' whose behaviour during the whole of the afternoon left much to be desired. A group of them found positions in a beer garden which backed onto the ground and they drank the afternoon away while watching the game without paying an entrance fee.

Their raucous noise level and the always underlying threat of jumping the fence and invading the pitch saw a total of five policemen and community policewomen, as well as club stewards, situated around the ground in order to be ready to prevent any problems. Alas, later in the evening many of them were involved in fighting and other disturbances in the King Street area of town. A number of arrests were made.

While all of this was going on the match had come to life in the second-half. Four goals in twenty minutes had seen the game go to extra-time. Then came the crunch for Carmarthen. As Aize said afterwards: "You know bad luck is running with you when, with four minutes of extra-time to play, you concede a weird goal."

"Prestatyn had a free kick from the right and a header towards goal bounced from the shoulders of two players and went in off the face of defender Tim Hicks. As a coach I just cannot legislate for incidents such as that."

During the half-time break, while a group of us were scoffing large slices of my wife's superb coffee cake, I saw Paul Fowler walking towards the back entrance holding his hand upwards. "It's my wrist," he said. He was taken to Glangwili Hospital; gave up after waiting for two hours to be seen by a doctor; was driven home by Geoff Kellaway and was then

Fowler injury

given treatment in Cardiff at his nearest Accident & Emergency Department.

"The downside to our exit from the Welsh Cup," said Aize, as reported in the *Carmarthen Journal*, "was that our inspirational midfielder, Paul Fowler, has broken his wrist and will be out of the game for at least eight weeks. However, this means that Paul's bad luck will open the door of opportunity for somebody else to step through."

Still, it was not all bad news for the club. In the Carmarthenshire League Challenge Cup semi-final the Reserves had beaten Pontarddulais 4-3, also after extra-time, to claim a spot in next month's final

The following afternoon the Academy team played Cambrian & Clydach, a side who were bottom of the Youth league. In quite a struggle the Old Gold won by a solitary goal. I spent part of the game with Alyth Jackson and the other with Roy Bergiers (Llanelli, Wales, British Lions). Although still involved in rugby, albeit at a junior level, he told me in some gruesome detail of the destruction of old records and memorabilia when Llanelli had moved from Stradey Park to Parc-y-Scarlets.

On the Wednesday of the week leading up to the away match against Port Talbot Town there was a meeting of representatives of southern Welsh Premier League clubs. I had been invited to attend and at the end of the evening found myself pleased to have been part of such a lively and productive discussion.

The chairman was Tony Bates (who holds the same position at Aberystwyth Town) and his control of the agenda was excellent. Whenever you have a quality chairman the level of debate always seems to rise as the meeting goes on. The main item up for discussion was the WPL Draft Strategy Document and the need for clubs to present a united front in reply.

After three very productive hours, agreement was reached on four major points. The first was the urgent need to increase the league to sixteen teams; then came the acceptance of the recommendation to promote clubs from the feeder leagues who finish in one of the top three positions; that it is strongly recommended to players that they take out their own personal insurance; and finally that a financial cap of £50,000 be put on the amount of money any individual can loan a club at any time.

Other than the chairman the other club representatives were Alan Howells (Afan Lido), Neil Dymock (Llanelli), Andrew Edwards (Port Talbot Town) and G.O. for Carmarthen. Whether the committee's views will be accepted in Cardiff is doubtful but at least an effort is being made.

The second weekend in March was scheduled to be busy, and it was. On the Friday evening we travelled the short distance to Victoria Road, Port Talbot to take on the team who were one place higher in the league than we were. A win would put us behind them by a point: defeat and we would start to be cast adrift of the pack.

As the match officials returned to the changing room from having refreshments in the clubhouse referee Richard Harrington asked Matthew Burgess and myself for the team list. We asked if it was possible to hold it for a few more minutes as Aize was in a secluded room with Paul Fowler and Welsh Referees' Manager Rodger Gifford.

When they emerged it was clear that Fowler had been refused permission to play. Keen as he was, the hard plaster cast on his wrist and lower right hand was considered dangerous. Rodger told me: "I examined the cast and told Paul that after he has it replaced with a soft polystyrene cast in about ten days time then he should come and see me again and I will make a decision then as to whether he can play or not."

However, none of this stopped the inspirational midfielder from warming up on the field with the rest of the team. It was interesting to note that when Liam McCreesh ran on to the pitch he hardly went twenty yards before walking back. "It's far too hard," he said. "I'm changing my boots." Four other players did likewise and somehow I felt that there were a few subconscious negatives around.

My fears translated themselves to the game which was turgid, to put it mildly. Ten minutes before the break a long high kick from the Port Talbot half of the field bounced over the head of Steve Cann who then slipped over. The hard pitch had a victim. Martin Rose (who had returned from financially stricken Llanelli) had the easiest of jobs to tap the ball into the net as Cann was even having difficulty getting to his feet. Four minutes later there was nearly a repeat but the subsequent shot was cleared away.

Defeat by a single goal was frustrating for the management team. Afterwards Kevin Morris was philosophical while Aize issued his weekly statement which, as always, praised his players for their efforts but realised that, for the immediate future, they had probably hit their ceiling. This was not a defeatist view but one which showed reality.

As he was keen on reminding people: "For a team who escaped relegation last season by the skin of their teeth, to now be in the League's top six and to have won silverware is quite an achievement."

Anyway success came the following day as Steve 'Gas's Reserve team had a 2-0 home win against Kidwelly which increased their lead at the top of the table.

The weekend saw the first gathering of groundhoppers for the year with the Ceredigion League hosting five games over two days. I met up with them at the Urdd Centre at Llangranog and after various greetings joined league secretary Geraint Davies and Crannog club officials for coffee. As soon as they saw the Carmarthen Town badge on my fleece the subject turned immediately to Iestyn Evans.

"We are so proud of him around here," said Crannog chairman Aled Roberts. "We have all seen him grow up and for a local lad to captain the Welsh Schools team is an honour felt by everyone."

Then, somehow, the name of G.O. cropped up. "I went to school with him," said Geraint Davies, "and when you get to St.Dogmaels you will find that most of the committee there are his relatives." What Geraint failed to add was that G.O. also had relatives at Maesglas and Llandysul Football Clubs as well. They breed robustly in these hills.

Lyn Brodrick, Iestyn Evans, Sam Wilson, Dafydd Jones and Ryan Stephens

The week leading up to yet another home game against Prestatyn Town saw the Academy team play a 2-2 draw with Afan Lido Youth. The match was not the best I have seen and for some reason the players seemed out of sorts. Admittedly it was a cold night but the enthusiasm just did not seem apparent. Iestyn Evans scored with an early header: two Carmarthen goalkeeping howlers let the visitors take the lead, before Gavin Rees equalised six minutes from time.

The day of yet another clash with Prestatyn started off as being clear and cold. By mid-morning the pitch at Richmond Park was perfectly playable: two hours later it was waterlogged. As Jonathan Lewis and Andrew Thomas sat helplessly in the main stand the rain poured down.

"I've never seen so much water on the pitch," said Michelle Hopkins as we looked out from the first floor window of the clubhouse. "It will be a wonder if we play today." The prognosis looked bad as the players of both sides started to appear. They milled around, not quite sure what to do. Referee Nick Pratt arrived and within a few minutes had changed and was inspecting the pitch. "I'll leave it an hour," he said, "and then make a decision."

During the hour's wait radio stations had to be fed information; various result services had to be told of the delay, while our secretary returned from the Cheltenham Festival having had considerable good fortune backing the horses. No wonder he was grinning inanely. Then came the final inspection following the hard work Jonathan, Andrew, and others had put into forking the pitch and clearing the surface water. "It's on," said Nick Pratt and the matchday wheels then started to turn.

Aize and Smudger gave the players their final briefing and the match finally got underway. Afterwards I told Aize that the players had got back their momentum which had been lost due to the break in

Jonathan Lewis and Andrew Thomas

fixtures."I could see it straight away," he said. "This was how I wanted them to play."

Play they did. Shot upon shot rained in on the Prestatyn goal: the pressure was immense. Finally the visiting defence broke as Corey Thomas, Liam McCreesh and Casey Thomas scored with other efforts being saved more by luck than judgement. Neil Gibson, the Prestatyn player-manager, whose suspension meant he had to sit in the stand, went wild at his player's performance. His choice of words were certainly not learnt from the pulpit.

The visitors changed their formation for the second-half, as did Carmarthen, who went on the defence. Both sides could easily have added to the score and although Prestatyn pulled back to 3-2 they never looked like taking a point. As the final whistle went I realised my feet were frozen and hands nearly numb. Never mind: we had got our first three points from the second phase of the season.

Four days later the FAW Youth Cup semi-final took place at Stebonheath Park in Llanelli. It was a cold night but that did not stop parents, their friends and Old Gold supporters from making the evening a good occasion.

When I wandered into the office Lucy Kelly was keying in names on the teamsheet and I could see that Peter Fearn had picked his strongest possible side. He had been quoted in the local 'paper saying: "We came through a very tough match in the last round. It is never easy playing in North Wales and some of the youngsters had to adjust quite quickly to Flint Town's robust style of play. This will stand them in good stead for this clash."

The Swansea City players gave off an easy air as they warmed up on what was a perfect pitch. They seemed to have more support staff than Carmarthen, which is not surprising considering the number of people employed at the club. Three months earlier they had been knocked out of the FA Youth Cup by Hull City so, in a way, this was a second bite of the cherry.

The first forty-five minutes saw Carmarthen pack their defence with only a weak effort from Callum Jackson troubling Swans 'keeper Oliver Davies. Sam Wilson limped off after twenty-four minutes to be replaced by Ross Jones. After the game Sam told me that he had a chronic exertional compartment syndrome injury which would need a lengthy amount of treatment from physiotherapist Matthew Lewis over the coming weeks.

Ten minutes after the break Sean Bergiers appeared to be tripped in the Swansea penalty area. I thought it a clear penalty but play was waved on. Twenty minutes later the same happened to Mitch Escott-Sloan. "Penalty" roared the crowd, and again I agreed with them. No way said referee Daniel Boyle.

By this time the Swans Youth team were two goals to the good; their first being the result of a goalkeeping blunder by our Portuguese goalkeeper Namir Queni, with the second coming from our exposed left back position. Swansea scored again near the end and the holders fully deserved their 3-0 victory.

There were lots of fun and games leading up to Saturday's postponed match against Airbus Broughton. My suspicions were raised on the Thursday afternoon when Rhys Felton sent me an email attaching a note he had received from the chairman of the Airbus Supporters Club. Both sets of supporters had arranged to play a game on a pitch at Trinity Fields (next to the Barn) starting at noon on the day of the match. The message relayed stated that the Airbus management had cancelled the fans' coach.

I sent the note to G.O. voicing my thoughts that maybe Airbus might not want to play the game due to the threat of adverse weather conditions. Like the reasons given for the Newtown postponement in early January, a number of the Airbus players and management lived in England where snow was forecast. This could well be the excuse?

On Friday morning Airbus indicated that they wanted to call the game off as it was snowing in Flintshire. G.O. looked at our pitch and, when asked by Andrew Howard, the FAW's Head of Competitions, informed him that it was perfectly playable. In mid-afternoon Andrew said the match should go ahead. At 6pm Airbus made a formal request for a postponement (ignoring the fact that we had a full clubhouse booking for sponsors' lunches). Forty-five minutes later an official WPL directive refused the request.

Then came the news that the match referee Bryn Markham-Jones would conduct a pitch inspection at 8.15 on Saturday morning. I felt sorry for him having to get up so early and drive to Carmarthen from Gorseinon. He duly arrived and declared the pitch perfectly playable.

While this was going on another request came from Airbus wanting the match called off on the grounds that their English "staff and players could not travel." I must confess to have had a wry smile at this as I was waiting for the usual crunch message. It arrived shortly afterwards. "Airbus cannot travel as their coach cannot get to the Airfield," said their statement.

Huge guffaws in my office with the comment being made that if Airbus were happy to be a Welsh Premier League club then surely they would have made provision for such an event. In all honesty it was poor behaviour with the result being that once again Carmarthen Town lost money for which there was no compensation.

The following day I went to Victoria Road to watch Port Talbot Town play The New Saints. Kevin Morris and Mark Aizlewood were both there and the three of us spent the day chatting to all and sundry. I joined some TNS supporters and asked about the depth of the snow on their pitch. "It's drifted to about head height," said one of the group. "We are situated on the Cheshire plain so that is why our immediate area is always likely to get drifting."

"What about next Saturday's match?" was my response. "Unlikely at the moment," I was told. "If we start moving the snow too early in the week it could melt, then freeze, even on our artificial surface."

On Thursday evening TNS posted requests on social media sites asking for supporters to attend the ground the following morning to help clear the pitch. G.O. was contacted and told that a decision would be made at noon on Good Friday as to whether the match would go ahead.

As I was going to North Wales anyway I took the opportunity to call in at Park Hall to see how the pitch clearance was going. To give the club their due, they were making a very good effort in somewhat trying circumstances. The match

Rhys Felton

would go ahead although as the owner, Mike Harris, told me: "It would not have taken place had there not been a partial thaw overnight which saw the height of the drifting snow considerably reduced."

As so happens when you meet football people our chat lasted over half an hour and covered a large number of WPL topics. I always find that I can learn so much from other points of view and Mike was generous with his time as I put innumerable questions to him. In the end I had to pull myself away, as I had an appointment with a book dealer in Wrexham, otherwise we would have gone on and on.

In the evening Mark Aizlewood and I went to The Airfield to see Airbus play Prestatyn. It gave me the opportunity to ask a few people about the previous weekend's situation and what I was told did clarify things in my mind. While Aize went and studied the Airbus team and tactics I found Andrew Lincoln, the club's media officer, to talk about his efforts in trying to get the WPL player details correct. The first ten years of record keeping had been somewhat inaccurate with Andrew telling me that only Connah's Quay's statistics were correct.

I arrived in Oswestry three hours before kick-off to find the Park Hall car-park and surrounding area full of vehicles. The leisure centre attached to the football ground had an ankle-biters Easter Bunny party in progress with the organisers having no idea that such an important football match was taking place.

I tried to explain to the ladies in charge that the game was being televised live and that should TNS beat Carmarthen then they would be crowned league champions. The look of utter bewilderment on their faces made me feel that maybe it was best they stuck to children while I would stick to football.

The team coach eventually made its way to the ground and the skill of the driver saw it reverse to within feet of the main entrance. Bags were unpacked and I was able to get the team details. *Radio Carmarthenshire* had time available during the afternoon's sports programme for me to be able to waffle for far longer than usual so I padded out the player details and gave some very esoteric statistics.

Gwyn Derfel sat next to me in the pressbox and I listened as he told the *S4/C* television producer about the procedure to be followed in the event of a presentation at the end of the game. There was no need to worry as Carmarthen did not spoil the party. In fact the Old Gold were so comprehensively beaten that the final 3-0 score was nowhere near a true reflection of what happened over the ninety minutes playing time.

To think that this was our fourth match against them this season and we had been unbeaten. That soon changed: not only were we unable to place a shot on-target but the two efforts off-target were well wide of the goal. Then Casey Thomas was given a straight red card on the hour mark which meant that we had reached a record four-hundred points mark on the WPL Fair Play Table. No team had ever before reached this mark: I wonder what will happen now?

Luxury Travel

Matthew Lewis

Colin Payne

On our travels

APRIL BLUES

April Fools' Day is celebrated in many countries. It is widely recognised and acclaimed as a day when people play practical jokes and hoaxes on each other. The earliest recorded association of an All Fool's Day, as it is sometimes called, was made in 1392. In the sixteenth century Pope Gregory XIII restored the Gregorian Calendar and made 1 April the day as we now know it.

This set me looking at the history of the Football Association of Wales. Was it founded on this day? Alas not: it turns out to be 2 February, albeit in 1876, when the Cambrian Football Association was formed at a meeting held at the Wynnstay Arms Hotel in Wrexham.

In the past my dealings with the FAW were on a professional footing and, as mentioned earlier in this book, I had the highest regard for the late Alun Evans and the way he ran the organisation. This regard has evaporated very quickly since I became involved with Carmarthen Town and I now share the complete exasperation as told to me by many involved with WPL clubs. It is not just WPL matters which have me frustrated beyond belief but also the virtual disdain in which Carmarthen Town and others are being treated in the run up to August's UEFA tournament.

In recent weeks there has been another meeting between the club, local government officials and other interested commercial bodies at which the FAW officials attended with considerable reluctance. Promises were made to the commercial sector which I know will not be met within the arranged proscribed time.

It was agreed then that a meeting would be held a few days later with representatives of all South West Wales newspapers and other media bodies. I duly turned up at the appointed time at the offices of the *Carmarthen Journal* along with people from Pembrokeshire and Ceredigion publications. I was talking with reporter Ian Lewis when the advertising manager, Gary Bacon (who had attended the original meeting), walked in to tell us that he had just received a message from the FAW to say that none of their representatives was going to be available. The subsequent views expressed were somewhat colourful.

It was suggested by Gary that we should try to arrange with the FAW for another time. Over the next few weeks Gary left voice-mail messages and sent emails trying to elicit even just a response from the FAW. All he had was silence.

At the meeting at which the FAW had originally attended, it was put to us that they would send the two female footballers, who had been nominated as the tournament's 'young ambassadors,' to Richmond Park. This would be for the scheduled home game against Airbus. Schools were contacted and they made arrangements for pupils from each to come to the game to meet the girls. Forty-eight hours before this was to take place the FAW announced that the girls "were unavailable."

It gets worse. The managers of St.Catherine's Walk (Mike Pugh) and Merlin's Walk (John Nash) were promised flags for lamp-posts; material bearing the UEFA logo and tournament information for other outdoor display and, with the offer of the use of an empty shop, items which could be put on tables to get the interest of the public. Both men had detailed schedules of events taking place in their respective Walks for over twelve months hence so needed to know what the FAW would be sending them. Utter silence to both.

Officials from both the Town Council and County Council, all of whom were clued up as to any role they could play in promotion and publicity, were getting nowhere with emails to Cardiff. Schools had been alerted but that was about all. The FAW told us that "tickets for the matches would be made available for distribution." Why bother, was my thought, as admission to games in Carmarthen would be free.

So, bearing all this in mind, on April Fools' Day I got to Richmond Park three hours before the scheduled start. It was the third attempt to play Airbus in the Championship Conference: surely nothing could go wrong today.

Andrew Thomas along with groundsman Jonathan Lewis, who had left his

Peter Hughes-Griffiths

sick bed to mark the pitch, had already been at the club for three hours. As G.O. was away he had asked me to meet and greet the match officials when they appeared. This left Huw Davies and myself to arrange the paperwork and to liaise with media outlets as is usual on a matchday.

Anthony Parnell arrived to carry out his role supervising the gatemen, ensuring the programmes were distributed and looking after security matters. Upstairs in the clubhouse, president Jeff Thomas had organised the lunch tables and was paying his usual special interest towards the day's sponsors.

In the changing room the kit had been laid out; practice and match balls put in their various places, with Keiran Davies preparing the cones and other paraphernalia needed for the players' warm-up session.

At 12.50pm I started to get concerned as no officials had arrived. Ten minutes later I tried to 'phone Gwyn Derfel only to find that he was on holiday for a week. Eventually contact was made with him and he tried from a distance to help but could not raise any official. In any case no fault lies with him as he does not make the referee's appointments.

By 1.15pm I was trying to make contact with the FAW Referees' Manager. He was eventually contacted by Mark Aizlewood at 2pm. To make matters worse the club's telephone lines were still out of order as they had been severed by a digging machine belonging to the contractor building the new changing rooms some three weeks earlier and had still not been repaired.

Ten minutes later I rang Alan Howells at Afan Lido to see if the officials for his match had arrived: they had. I asked him if he could persuade the fourth official to travel to Carmarthen to officiate. I already had two first grade linesmen available, if needed. The fourth official refused the request which he was entitled to do.

Then the idea occurred to me to try and contact the officials originally appointed for the postponed game. None replied to any calls although it was said later that a friend of the referee had spoken to him twice and on both occasions had denied knowing of any appointment for the afternoon.

Then it was a matter of trying to phone anyone from the FAW who might be able to help. Another blank. Meanwhile John Gow, the referees's assessor, had turned up. In discussion with him he admitted that it was unusual not to have been told prior to the game as to who the officials were but he thought it was just someone being forgetful.

At 2.10pm Aize received a call from Rodger Gifford saying: "Postpone the game." While this was happening the reporter from *BBC Radio Cymru*, sitting cold and alone in the stand, had made contact with someone from the FAW to be told that no one was authorised to postpone the match.

Malcolm Williams

Mike Davies then decided to interview both managers for *Sgorio* with each being as irate as the other. Andy Preece felt that his team's chances of consolidating second position in the WPL had been affected while Aize spoke about the lack of communication between FAW personnel.

In the clubhouse Jeff Thomas was fuming. "All these people have come for lunch,"he said. "They have had a good meal along with plenty to drink. I can't charge them for any of this as a match was included in the package. Once again we have taken another financial hit." Added to Jeff's woes the match programmes, printed for the original fixture, could not be used; there were no takings from the burger bar; the loss of a Bank Holiday crowd (possibly 280 x £7) from pay at the gate spectators was substantial, and who knows what sales would have been made from the Club Shop.

A person with considerable financial nous told me: "With the Connah's Quay fiasco; Newtown and Airbus refusing to travel to scheduled matches, and now this FAW cock-up, I have tried to look at the club's business plan with a view to assessing the overall loss. In my opinion it is a fraction shy of £10,000." On the pitch Aize will tell you that the momentum the team had gained had all but been lost.

Later in the afternoon Gwyn Derfel said: "It is embarrassing for the league, but all I can say is that normal procedures for reappointing officials to the game were not followed."

Then came a joint statement from the FAW and WPL: "The WPL would like to apologise for the fact that the Easter Monday match was postponed. It was rescheduled during the recent adverse weather and on this occasion ..... blah, blah, blah." The excuses rambled on and on. Then the FAW tried to put the blame on to G.O. for not contacting the officials prior to the game. If no one had been appointed then how was he to contact them? Anyway, what had the weather to do with someone sitting in a heated Cardiff office being unable to make appointments?

I gave the *South Wales Evening Post* a few quotes to use followed by Aize saying: "It's very disappointing because my players were ready; the Airbus players were also ready, and the club officials were ready, but there is nothing we can do."

Brian Davies

Stewart Roberts, the Airbus chief operating officer was incensed by the blunder. "Someone, somewhere, is to blame. We will leave it to the powers-that-be to find out the circumstances behind this embarrassing situation. That said, someone will have to pay the travel costs and wages for players in attendance and the league will seriously need to look at how they ensure Airbus are not financially penalised for this in any way."

I felt like contacting Stewart to tell him that he had a snowball's chance in hell of getting any compensation. If we were £10,000 down the pan due to mismanagement and lack of strong leadership then how does he think he will get £3,000? Poor deluded boy.

Over the next few days I enjoyed reading through comments being placed on internet chat-rooms. One (a vicar from Pontypool with whom I am acquainted) wrote: 'Surely there is somebody from the WPL on standby who could have found a qualified referee in the locality. Even if they had had to bring Welsh League standard officials from the Swansea area and delayed the kick-off, it would have been better than sending Airbus all the way back home without the match being played."

Someone else wondered about compensation for the clubs which quickly had the retort: "Yes, but what about compensation for the fans?" Another pointedly said: "People often ask on this forum why a number of Welsh clubs prefer to play in England. Do you now understand?"

Elsewhere, on another thread, a Welsh based football director wrote: "The sad thing is that for seasoned observers of Welsh football this news will be received without surprise or anger. It is an everyday tale of the sort of bungling incompetence and lack of communication and accountability which is the normal way of things at FAW-lty Towers, Cardiff Bay. Watching the two managers being interviewed on *Sgorio* we saw from them the same hopelessness that things would never change."

He continued: "There will be no compensation because there never is. Neither will there be any FAW official disciplined or replaced; there never is. They will go on doing things their way oblivious of the consequences to football in the Principality." He finished with the view: "Those English football officials reading this who are tempted to complain about the Football Association or your local County FA - Just think yourselves lucky."

Probably the best assessment of Welsh football governance came from a respected Oxfordshire sports writer. "I think this all goes to show that the FAW seem to have problems with very simple logistical and administrative tasks."

Looking at the elected representatives he commented: "Many in the organisation think they do a good job; try to say they are only in that job because no one else wants it or there is no one else willing to do it. But if anyone else was willing or wanted those jobs the people in situ would do their utmost to make it impossible for those interested to get to those positions. Until something drastic happens heads will remain in the sand or up backsides and the buck will never stop."

I read those and other points of view with considerable interest little realising what would happen next.

"You're going deaf," said my wife. "Go and get your ears syringed." That was the reason I was sitting in the doctor's waiting room on Wednesday morning reading an article about America in some woman's magazine. I had hardly started it when a Carmarthen Town supporter walked in; saw me, and wanted to know what had gone on. As I started telling him I realised that everyone was listening. No one moved until the story was over. Then came the questions which were only interrupted by the doctor calling out a patient's name. None of them could comprehend the farce behind the narrative.

At training that night G.O. mentioned to me that Airbus were proposing rearranging our home and away fixtures with them. What was being suggested would cause us massive inconvenience. In any case, for our trip north on Saturday, G.O. had provisionally booked hotel rooms for Friday evening while Aize had arranged to use Wrexham's training ground in Gresford on Saturday morning.

Aize got the players together and spelt out the logistics for travel on Friday. There would be an allowance for the use of each car plus all petrol

Nicky Palmer & Mark Aizlewood

and expenses would be met by the club. Then he and Smudger went and detailed the tactics to be used for the away match, which always differ from those when we are playing at home. There was even time for me to give Nicky Palmer a copy of the *Carmarthen Journal* which contained a photograph and an article about his one hundredth WPL appearance for the Old Gold.

The following morning as I was sitting at the breakfast table, eating my way through a large bowl of porridge, the mobile 'phone burped out its noise. It was G.O. at the other end. "We are playing at home on Saturday," he said, "and going up to Airbus on Tuesday evening. It is a decision forced on us by the Welsh Premier League Panel and there is nothing we can do about it."

Not long after Aize was told the news came the not unexpected response from the players. Paul Fowler could not play because of the hard plastercast on his wrist; Casey Thomas was suspended; Tim Hicks and Matthew Rees would be out of the country; others could not get time off work at such short notice while Aize himself was going to be in London on business.

At the first count four players were available. By late that night it had risen to five. The only answer was to see if any of the reserve team could play in what would be their one and only WPL appearance. Thank goodness I wasn't involved in sorting out yet another mess imposed on us from above.

On Reflection ....

During Thursday afternoon G.O. left the club office to go to his bank for a scheduled appointment. On the way he bumped into Ceri Stennett and Peter Barnes of the FAW who told him that they had just left a meeting held in the offices of the *Carmarthen Journal*. When this was relayed to me I was virtually speechless as no one had told me it was taking place.

I contacted Gary Bacon to see if he had been involved and he too expressed considerable annoyance as he still had heard nothing from Cardiff. He promised to investigate and duly came back with the news that a reporter had seen them, by request, and that the only discussion had revolved around getting a weekly column in the news section of the paper each week until the tournament was over at the end of August.

The following day I contacted the FAW and to say I was ear-bashed would be putting it mildly. What I was told was arrogant in the extreme: I was informed that, *inter-alia*, we were country folk who did not understand what the city-slickers were organising. "Leave it to us," I was told. "We'll have stuff ready for your town traders by July."

July! Now what? Do we tell Mike Pugh and John Nash? Do we whisper in the ears of Town and County council officials? Do we still involve the schools? Do we do our own thing? Somehow the mess which is being created must not reflect badly on Carmarthen Town. Let's get this Airbus farce out of the way and then make some decisions.

I thought I would be the first person to arrive at Richmond Park on the first Saturday of April but, as usual, I was beaten to it by Aize (who was drawing the day's tactics on the office whiteboard), Andrew and Jonathan (who were putting up the goalnets and marking the pitch) and the *Sgorio* camera crew.

Soon the matchday wheels started to crank into motion; the players arrived in dribs and drabs, and Airbus officials appeared in the clubhouse. They are a friendly group of people and I never fail to get into a chat with Ian Cowell about any of our surplus programmes which they could have for their Club Shop.

Today all went smoothly. The officials had been appointed correctly (albeit from North Wales which cost us hundreds of pounds in expenses) and a surprise visitor was Rodger Gifford, the FAW Referee's Manager. But to cap it all my wife had baked chocolate cakes (note the plural) which made the media centre quite a popular place during the afternoon.

Gareth Davies

The coaching team must have been quietly satisfied with the players' performance during the ninety minutes of play. A goal by Corey Thomas after twenty-two minutes, direct from a left side free-kick, gave the Old Gold three valuable points in their chase for fifth spot in the league.

"I wanted that win to prove a point," said Aize. "We are being stuffed up big-time for the return match and I needed to show that my team were capable of beating Airbus." What he did not know then was that the WPL decision to make Carmarthen play at home with just forty-eight hours notice had resulted in the lowest crowd at Richmond Park for many, many years.

When he got in front of the *Sgorio* cameras, Airbus manager Andy Preece found the defeat too much to take so he spent the whole of his interview slagging off the quality of the pitch. It was so repetitive a moan that only a few clips were of use for the final broadcast. Sitting in on the filming was webmaster Huw Davies and afterwards he challenged Preece over his views. Their 'discussion' did not reach a mutually satisfying conclusion.

Then it was time to see if anything could be made of the mess made by the WPL Panel. I joined Aize, Anthony Parnell and Paul Ashley-Jones in discussing how many first-team players were now available for Tuesday and where were we going to find any others. To make matters worse Liam Thomas had been injured during the afternoon so that looked like one less available body.

All names were written down. After various 'phone calls were made there were five first-team; one Reserve team, and two Academy players available to travel north. There seemed no way we would be able to get eleven players on to the pitch. We were joined by Peter Fearn, Steve 'Gas,' and Keiran Davies in order to go through the logistics. Peter would drive the minibus and coach the side: it would all be a nonsense.

Behind the scenes emails were flowing in all directions. The WPL hierarchy (which really means the elderly FAW councillors) were holding firm: their stubbornness showing why many consider the league to be little more than a sad joke. The publicity they could expect to receive in the Welsh Monday morning newspapers would not be pleasant reading. Was anyone going to give ground?

The internet proved its worth over the next couple of days. The vitriol hurled by football bloggers was a sight to behold. Even normally compliant commentators were having a field day. I did nothing to discourage them, in fact I sent background briefing notes to every source I knew within the Welsh sports media. Some took my bait: others didn't.

Jeff Thomas understands politics in all its senses. Our president found himself sending emails of protest to Cardiff while also trying to stop the club being humiliated on the field of play. The number of first-team players

Jenny Williams & Eirlys Thomas

139

available to get to the game rose to eight of whom Liam Thomas and Academy player Sam Wilson would play against medical advice. Of course, both couldn't last the pace: Sam played twenty minutes while Liam hobbled off later on.

Mark Aizlewood was going to be in London directing business training courses. The thought of missing the game and not being with his team became too much for him. He sent me a text: "I'm going," he wrote. "I have a chauffeur driven car booked to take me from Harrow to Euston. I then take a train to Crewe; change for Chester and another chauffeur to take me to the ground. I'll be there at 7.15pm." As it happened he arrived twenty minutes early. He stayed overnight in Chester and then caught the 5.30am train back to London the next morning.

Jeff Thomas was also away from home on business. He was in Aberystwyth and decided that he should attend the game. He drove to Welshpool and hitched a lift on the minibus from there. On arrival at the Chester Road ground it was found that Carmarthen had twelve players, three of whom would be in the starting eleven for the first time. On the substitutes bench would be Finton O'Brien, normally a reserve team player.

When I spoke to Aize the following afternoon he sounded knackered but was a proud man. "They were magnificent," he told me. "We had a shot hit the post before they scored; we had another effort cleared off the line and McCreesh missed a sitter. We played the last quarter of the match with ten men and to lose by only 2-0 was a credit to all of those who made such an effort to be there."

What I thought wise not to mention was that I had been at Richmond Park to see Steve Gas's side take on Abergwili. A twelfth minute volley by centre-back Jody Thomas not only won the game for the Old Gold but also gave them the Carmarthenshire League Second Division championship. Alas it was not all success as two days later defeat in the semi-final of the Mond Cup, albeit by penalties, saw the team's first loss of the season.

Namir Queni

As I was going to be in North Wales for the weekend I thought I would drop in on Friday evening to see TNS play Airbus on the 3G pitch at Park Hall in Oswestry. It was an ideal opportunity to talk to officials of both clubs about current issues. What I quickly found out was that the WPL Panel which condemned Carmarthen to play away at Airbus with a few hours notice was an FAW gathering in disguise. It would seem that the three WPL club representatives on the seven man panel knew nothing of the meeting.

As the evening wore on so the stories, news and gossip got even better. The fact that TNS were tearing Airbus to pieces took second preference to the background briefings my ears were hearing. A number of things were now clearer in my mind, even down to who the match officials should have been at our April Fool's Day débâcle had they been properly informed.

Finton O'Brien

The following morning I was in Bangor and with time on my hands took the opportunity to walk around the pedestrianised centre. There was an undercurrent of poverty all around and a considerable attitude problem among the roaming bands of youths. Yet the books for sale in the Oxfam shop were of a high quality: such is the dichotomy of it also being a University town.

I arrived at the football ground at the same time as the *Sgorio* camera crew. As the players had stayed locally overnight they started to arrive by the carload which threw the cameraman who was waiting for a coach to appear. Once I had our team selection it was 'phoned through to Ollie Cole at *Radio Carmarthenshire* so we could prepare for my preview report.

Everything ran smoothly for me during the afternoon. On the field the Old Gold conceded an early goal, following a schoolboy error in the defence, but then held out until the virtual last kick of the match before letting Bangor in for a second. "It has been a very difficult week for the players," said Aize after the game. "They performed well today and only a 2-0 defeat shows that we are within touching distance of the top three teams. The progress we have made this season is phenomenal."

Unfortunately the day was spoilt for me by the strange and aggressive behaviour of a club steward. I was sitting in the pressbox between the *BBC Radio Cymru* broadcaster and Dave Jones (*Daily Post*). As they were both busy I decided to hold giving my final radio report and was talking about the game with John Collyer. For some reason, and I really do not know what it was, this steward ran up the stairs and started yelling at me. Startled, I told him to go away which made him more aggressive and he started trying to hit me until other stewards arrived to pull him away. It's never any good trying to complain about these sort of people as you never get anywhere. It reminded me of something my old sociology professor drummed into me years ago.

"Never argue with the lower classes," he told our tutorial group, "for they are always right and never wrong."

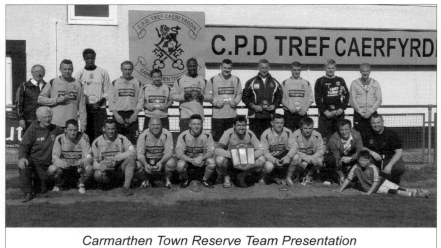

Carmarthen Town Reserve Team Presentation

The rearranged home fixture with The New Saints took place on a Tuesday night in mid-April. The ground still resembled a building site with a trench having been dug outside the Priory Street turnstiles and a large area of the terraces cordoned off. Even the burger bar was closed and out of bounds. Progress on the new changing rooms was going well even though the contract with the builder had stipulated an end of March completion time.

The attraction of the newly crowned league champions meant that a quality sponsor had booked all available spaces for dinner. Macron were the kit suppliers to the club and their host for the evening was Ray Pennock a man whose claim to fame is that he had scored Carmarthen Town's very first top flight goal. (To be accurate, it was achieved in the thirtieth minute of the 2-0 away win against Briton Ferry Athletic on 17 August 1996).

Everywhere else people were slotting into place. Paul Evans had taken up his customary position at the clubhouse turnstiles with Clive Evans looking after those at the St.Peter's car-park side. Geraint Hughes was back on the tannoy following his quadruple heart bypass operation while I was chasing around trying to find programme contributor Alun Charles. Committeeman Clive Thomas was preparing the season ticket and vice-presidents' lists for next season as Paul Ashley-Jones was distributing information for the club's end-of-season fete.

In the matchday office, thanks to the good efforts of John Davidson, we now had a broadband connection albeit a temporary measure prior to our summer move to a new residence on the other side of the ground. Huw Davies had brought along all of the necessary computer equipment in case we were having problems: we weren't but Gil Woolley, the TNS media officer, was more than grateful to be able use some of it.

Ray Pennock

Before the game we were joined by WPL secretary Gwyn Derfel who had a lengthy conversation with John Collyer and myself concerning the outrageous behaviour of the club steward at Bangor a few days earlier. After that I trailed over to the media centre carrying bags containing tins of my wife's jam & cream sponge cake which did rather weigh me down. When I arrived the expectant look on the faces of those already in situ was of spoilt anticipation. As Mick Evans joined us for the first time in ages he had first choice of the largest slices: after that the vultures pounced.

The match was a splendid example of how far Aize and Smudger had taken the team in such a short while. They ran and fought for every ball; the tackling was perfect; and the pressure put on the TNS defence was outstanding. Yes, TNS did win the game with a tapped in goal ten minutes from the end, but they are full-time professional players who, at the final whistle, dropped down in exhaustion.

I was proud of their performance as were all those around me. Later on, in the clubhouse, the feeling was one of satisfaction. Aize took me to one side: "We have got this far in leaps and bounds, Chris. Now people have got to understand that progress is an inch by inch movement."

The final home league fixture of the season was against Port Talbot Town. Initially we were a bit concerned that their usually small, but raucous, group of supporters might attend but in the end less than a dozen of them turned up. The visitors had nothing to play for as they had consolidated fourth position in the WPL whatever the result.

As I said on air to various radio stations during the match: "The game started badly and went downhill from then on." Aize took a different line saying: "I make no apologies for the nature of our performance as we needed to get a point."

Maybe he was right but in any case it was a drab afternoon made even

Geraint Hughes

worse by the fact that media commitments resulted in my having to forgo Bernie Davies's kind invitation to join him at his sponsored (by A.T.B.Davies Haulage Contractors') lunch table. The anticipation of our little group having a meal meant that my wife had not prepared any cake for the afternoon, a situation seized upon by Aize who complained loudly to all and sundry. He was temporarily satiated by a large tin of chocolate biscuits being thrust in front of him. However, a compromise was reached with my wife a few days later when she promised to make him his own favourite coconut cake for the next home game.

Fortunately the scoreless draw was enlivened by an enormous amount of gossip from around the media centre. I was able to relate stories heard the previous night at Afan Lido, when they had played an equally awful end-of-season match against Aberystwyth Town, and in turn was told of some of the latest shenanigans around which Welsh football is built. The self importance of certain individuals would be hilarious if it wasn't so sad.

The afternoon's draw had moved us into fifth position on the WPL table. As Prestatyn Town, our nearest league challengers, had been thrashed 7-1 at home by TNS our goal difference suddenly was four goals better even though both clubs had the same number of points. Aize said: "We now go to Prestatyn next Saturday and just need to avoid defeat to claim a home tie in the Europa League qualifying semi-final."

The mood in the clubhouse was very upbeat. I sat with Howard Williams, (the other) Gareth Jones and Alan Latham as we tried to work out the possible scenario for our May fixtures. Anthony Parnell was taking the names of those wishing to go to Prestatyn on the mini-bus while quite a number seemed to have made their own arrangements for Friday night accommodation along the North Wales coast.

The next day my wife and I went to have Sunday lunch at Ceredigion's

famous *Emlyn Cafe* in Tanygroes. While the owner Lyn Evans was out delivering Meals-on-Wheels we got chatting to Malcolm Davies who mentioned that they were both staying in the same Halkyn motel in which I, along with all of the players, had been booked. I have a feeling that Saturday morning's breakfast in the dining room of the nearby Springfield Hotel will be full of chatter.

Midweek saw the Carmarthen Academy team finish their home fixtures with a draw against Aberdare and a single goal loss to West End. Since the cup semi-final defeat the heart seemed to have gone out of their game and many of the team played their final match at Richmond Park.

Lyn Evans

The week also brought news from the High Court in London that Llanelli Football Club had been wound up. For all of their protestations the club had been living on borrowed time for ages. The best case scenario for them now is to reform and try to get admitted into the third division of the Welsh League, although there is even doubt about that being allowed by the FAW.

At the Afan Lido match I had bumped into Tony Bates who mentioned in passing that there was to be a meeting of the WPL Panel on Thursday. He told me that the first item on the Agenda was 'Airbus/Carmarthen Matches,' and wondered if the club might like to make any comment. With the agreement of G.O. I submitted the first part of this chapter for his consideration. I wonder how it will be received?

In the meantime the internet bloggers were having their say about the demise of Llanelli. "The foundation of the League of Wales was always going to be an unsustainable concept," wrote one well known scribe. "We all knew from the start it would eventually self destruct. That was why the clubs based in the English leagues fought so hard to stay where they were. They knew what would happen."

I travelled north on the last Friday in April through all of the four seasons. I left Carmarthen in the warmth; car windows open and music my grandmother called "sinful" belching loudly from the tape-deck. By Rhayader the cold wind had taken over; the windows were closed and the heater was going full blast. Soon after leaving Newtown it started to snow and by the time I got to Oswestry it was necessary to put on warmer clothing.

Eventually I arrived in Corwen in good time for the evening's Welsh National League Premier Division match against Brymbo. I enjoy watching football in Denbighshire and expected a quiet time. No such luck: I think it has something to do with the Carmarthen Town embossed badge on my fleece.

With a number of committee people from nearby Bala Town wanting to hear about the Old Gold's various problems over recent weeks, through to explaining in detail the Llanelli situation, meant that I was able to watch fairly little of the game. However, the good side of an evening's solid gossip was finding out a non-football story which was soon sold on to a London newspaper.

By mid-evening I had arrived at the Travelodge in Halkyn which is my usual base for visits to North Wales. The car-park was full so I guessed most of the team had arrived. The next door cafe had only two customers so I asked at reception if the players had wandered down to the nearby Red Lion hotel. I was completely taken aback when told that they were in their rooms. Over the years I have travelled with football, rugby and cricket teams and witnessed situations which get better with constant retelling as we all get older.

An hour before midnight the motel went quiet. I sat reading in my room, waiting for either a lot of noise or, at a minimum, the fire-alarms being set off. I fell asleep and was only woken in the morning by a call on my mobile 'phone. Where were the players? The receptionist told me they had already left for a training session at the nearby Halkyn United ground. I was taken

aback. What is happening to today's youth? They seem so conservative. Or is it that I am just an old git whose youthful excesses were part of a generation now long extinct.

As I entered the Pentre Road ground I could see the players going through various routines on the pitch. The morning was warm and visibility good. The view over the pitch towards the estuary of the River Dee was idyllic; in fact it was a perfect place to watch football. I got chatting to Brian Pugh, the Halkyn United secretary and he spent time explaining where improvements were going to be made and a clubhouse erected.

I joined physiotherapist Matthew Lewis on the touchline and we watched as Aize and Smudger explained the day's tactics. The ideas were good but I did wonder if more time was needed to perfect the thoughts behind them. Later, in talking with Aize, I told him about a conversation I had had years earlier with a former manager, Neil Warnock. He told me: "When I coach Premiership players I teach them a routine on a fortnightly basis. With Football League players you do it weekly; In the Football Conference it's twice a week, while in non-league it's every training session." I think his point was valid.

The players then broke off for breakfast while I went to explore junk shops along the coast. As the kick-off was not going to be until late afternoon I had plenty of time to rummage through a lot of dross but did have success in finding a couple of nineteenth century books.

The Prestatyn Town ground is situated on a raised beach four hundred yards from the sea. In between is Prestatyn Cricket Club where I idled away an hour watching a Liverpool Combination match. Soon it was time to concentrate on football and within a few minutes of entering the ground radio producer Emyr James was on the 'phone to discuss the afternoon's reports.

Then came an important part of the afternoon: the distribution of my wife's cakes to the hungry hordes. Lyn Evans and Malcolm Davies were waiting patiently in a car for the offerings and as soon as they had helped themselves so a minibus driven by Bernie Davies pulled up. The ravenous faces at the bus windows stared longingly into the tins containing cappuccino flavoured iced cake. A few minutes later and I was putting empty tins back into my car.

Once the team news had been given out on radio I went and stood by the entrance to the pitch and was joined by Mark Hannington, Andrew Thomas and Jonathan Lewis. As we chatted so Aize came over and very soon he was relating a hilarious story about a dwarf, none of which I would dare mention here.

The match came and went. Prestatyn won 2-1 to claim fifth position in the league but no Carmarthen supporter could have asked for more from the team. The effort they put it was top rate and the final twenty minutes saw a siege laid on the home goal. Shot upon shot rained in; corner after corner was gained; free kicks were put high into the penalty area with many finding the head of defender Matthew Rees, but all to no avail.

Because of media commitments I did not leave Bastion Gardens until an hour after the final whistle. Halfway home the 'phone rang. It was Aize. "I was proud of them today," he said. "I find it very difficult to be critical as they are an honest, trustworthy bunch of lads who give their all, week in, week out. They have been absolutely magnificent from day one and I'm proud to be their coach."

I could only but agree with his assessment. However, now the league season had finished it was time to look towards the Europa League play-off matches. We would be playing away whatever happened elsewhere.

Alun Charles

The Sunday lunches are superb

Mick Evans

Training at Halkyn

WINDING DOWN

The first day of May saw the release of the season's Welsh Premier League crowd figures. They did not make for good reading. On his website Andrew Lincoln wrote as follows:

'WPL attendances went into freefall this season dropping by more than 15%, the largest decrease in the league's twenty year history. The average attendance at the 192 games was just 279, compared to 329 in 2011/12.'

'Leading the way were Bala Town whose gates fell by 34%; Afan Lido 28% and champions, The New Saints, who saw a drop of nearly a quarter in the average Park Hall crowd. There were also significant decreases at Port Talbot Town (22%) and Llanelli (17%). Only two clubs increased their attendances. Airbus Broughton's best-ever season brought 36% more spectators through the turnstiles, while Newtown attracted 26% more.'

'Gates are now only marginally better than they were in the last season of the eighteen-club league when an average of 276 spectators attended each game. There were 306 fixtures played in that 2009/10 campaign with 84,482 fans attending matches compared with just 53,545 in the season just ended.'

Andrew went on to say that this evidence supported the claims that the current format, with its mid-season split, did not have much appeal. He cited the views of our own Jeff Thomas, and the Aberystwyth Town manager Tomi Morgan, both of whom had been very vocal on the matter.

Reading all the data Andrew put with his article made me wonder as to how low the figures had to get before it dawned on the FAW that the system they had forced on the clubs was not fit for purpose. Is the whole reason for the current set-up purely to allow clubs to play one European home game each season?

In a recent Haverfordwest County programme, secretary Barry Vaughan reported in some detail on the discussion held at a meeting of the Welsh League. He said that the clubs did not have either the facilities or infrastructure to make any application for a WPL Domestic Licence nor did they have the finances to spend on ground improvements which, in reality, would mostly remain unused.

He was very clear in stating that he could not see any club in South Wales, other than his own, "being able to meet the demands of the Domestic Licence in the near future, or even wanting to." Like many, he feared that the WPL would become a North Wales dominated league, "with the consequential

Emlyn Schiavone

massive increase in travel costs dominating the southern clubs' finances."

The report, by Tony Bates, of the WPL Panel meeting duly found its way on to my desk. I read it with increasing incredulity before passing it over to my wife for her thoughts. While reading it she burst out laughing, saying: "It's like one of those Brian Rix farces which we used to see on television years ago. You couldn't make it up and if you did no one would believe it to be true."

Alas, it was true: all of it. So as not to cause any feeling of betraying confidences or embarrassment to any of the WPL club representatives I shall just mention one small point. On the issue of the non-attendance of officials for our home match with Airbus, comment came from on high admitting that: "... a significant amount of blame lay with the FAW who had not confirmed the appointments."

In a final personal paragraph to the clubs who he represents, Tony Bates wrote: "There is no question the FAW needs younger faces and brighter minds .... and I was not surprised to be told that of the thirty-five FAW councillors, four are residing in nursing homes."

With all but the first-team having completed their programme it was possible to look back at what had taken place over the past few months. Steve Gas's Carmarthenshire League side had won the Second Division Championship and had remained unbeaten in the league over the whole season. They had lost in the Challenge Cup Final by a single goal and were knocked out of the Mond Cup on penalties in the semi-final.

Peter Fearn's Academy team had not had a good league campaign compared to the previous year. They had won only four of their eighteen matches although finishing with a positive goal difference. The FAW Youth Cup run to the semi-final had been a success but now many of the players were now going to be over-age and would be missing from next season's squad.

The big surprise for Aize's team was Prestatyn Town winning the FAW Cup. This meant that the Europa League Qualifying semi-final would now be away at Port Talbot Town.

Prior to Wednesday training the players went into the matchday office to sign various bits of official paperwork. While they were there I got them to fill out a questionnaire which I needed for a 'Player Profile' section of the programme I am preparing for next season. Some of the answers were most revealing with occupations ranging from Company Director to International Banking Officer; Residential Care Worker; Teacher, and on to various trade positions.

Quite a few gave North Wales as an answer to "I never want to go there again," with hobbies and interests being dominated by other sports, particularly golf. The more senior players generally chose reading with politics, music and television documentaries also mentioned.

The evening also threw up some odd questions. G.O. was fussing about whether all the players had passports just in case we won the next two matches. Aize remarked about training continually if we did get into European competition while G.O. was frazzled after a day welcoming representatives from the countries taking part in August's UEFA tournament. "We will need interpreters," he commented. "I hope the FAW will supply them."

But what I did like was a Twitter comment from Christian Doidge later on in the evening as he was being driven home: "Falling asleep in the back of the car listening to Geoff Kellaway and Paul Fowler talking about changing nappies."

The weather was overcast as I made my way along the motorway to Port Talbot. The gates to the football ground were open and I was able to park behind the main stand. Only a few people were milling around but in the away changing room Gareth Davies was putting out the kit in neat piles. Gary Morris arrived and was soon massaging Craig Hanford's back problem; Steve 'Gas' was out on the pitch setting up cones for the pre-match warm-up session while Kevin Morris, Neil Smothers and Mark Aizlewood were discussing the final team tactics.

Soon it was time to exchange teamsheets, with opposing manager Scott Young very keen to see our line-up. He would have been completely bamboozled by seeing defender Carl Evans at centre-forward with no Liam Thomas or Geoff Kellaway in the side. "We have no pace up-front," said Aize reflecting on what might have been had the players been available for selection.

Gareth Jones

As mentioned earlier in this book the Port Talbot pressbox is probably the best on the circuit. I joined Matthew Burgess and Rob Clement, the usual occupiers, along with Gwyn Derfel who you sense prefers the company of journalists during a match rather than being officially on duty and listening to the moans of club officials.

The first half saw both sides cancel each other out. Before the start I had mentioned to Liam McCreesh about a Twitter comment that someone had put £10, at 10/1, on him getting a red card: he already knew about it. After eighteen minutes referee Nick Pratt waved a yellow card in front of McCreesh which set the pressbox into speculation. Further warnings followed but he survived until substituted.

I really do not know what it is with our matches against Port Talbot. Whenever they score against us it is usually a weird deflection or a playground error. Their goal in this game was no exception to the rule. A left wing through ball was collected by captain David Brooks whose angled shot hit Paul Fowler who was standing on the goal-line. It smacked him on the chest and spun back into the net. That one slice of fate ended our season, and any potential interest in European competition.

Afterwards I found Aize sitting in an easy chair in the boardroom. "I keep being asked about the match," he said, "but what concerns me more is to tell these people about the achievements of the playing staff who have been absolutely magnificent."

"My players have shown their ability on the field of play and put up a fantastic performance to only lose by a solitary goal. They have proved once again the spirit they have for the cause of Carmarthen Town Football Club. The big challenge now facing them is to keep going forward."

Sam Wilson & Iestyn Evans

As he finished my 'phone started ringing. Various radio stations wanted match reports and a round-up of the season; the *Mid-Glamorgan Sports Agency* asked for copy, and out of the blue *Wales on Sunday* wanted five hundred words. An hour later I had completed all the tasks. I could drive back to my office while reflecting on the past ten months. Even when I got back there was no peace. The previous week Emlyn Schiavone had organised his annual Primary Schools' football tournament and the day's photographs had arrived in my computer system but with no captions or text. It was not until late the following day could they all be dispatched to the *Carmarthen Journal*.

Because of my past involvement in sports history and sports science I still get a lot of academic studies sent to me. Three have come recently which have a minor, but interesting, relevance to the Welsh Premier League.

All of them were looking at comparisons. The first one had made an analysis of attendance figures and the author quoted 'Leo's Law' (named after Leo Hoenig, who had originally studied the concept) which states: "Leagues of a similar average attendance are usually of similar ability."

This had been taken up by the second study which made comparisons of various football leagues. In part it said: "The standard of the WPL is somewhere between the Scottish Football League Second and Third Divisions," adding "that the WPL compares well to the Southern League Premier Division."

However, the third, and best, came from Cardiff Metropolitan University. They had copied the concept first used at Loughborough University by comparing games reel by reel in unison. The report covered numerous games but I will pick out one which looked at the WPL against the Football Conference. The matches, played on the same day fifty miles apart were Prestatyn Town versus Port Talbot Town, and Stockport County versus Woking.

After various preliminaries it said: "The difference was striking in two respects in particular. First, the time players got on the ball to decide what to do next and, secondly, the speed with which the Conference teams could get the ball from one end of the pitch to the other."

In defence of the WPL the writer added: "We watched quite a number of their matches on our monitor screens and they can be quite enjoyable on their own terms, partly because players do get much more time to think and that teams lack the fitness to cancel each other completely out as can happen in the Conference. However, we would state that in our opinion the WPL players who could make the step up between the two leagues would be few and far between."

The report commented further: "One more pointer might be that Airbus, who signed quite a number of players from the Conference, finished in second place on the WPL, beaten only by a full-time side with the advantage of a plastic pitch."

Craig Hanford & Mark Aizlewood

Ian Hillier & Neil Smothers

The third Monday in May saw the club's Management Committee convene its usual monthly meeting. Before that took place the Directors had met with representatives of a company who are involved with 3G pitches in order to get a better idea of the benefits, or otherwise, of having such a playing surface. As they spoke contractors were digging up our grass pitch in order to get it relaid and in perfect order for the forthcoming UEFA tournament.

The Management meeting really opened my eyes to the amount of work which goes into the club's Academy. Keiran Davies spoke eloquently about the under age teams and the running costs involved. The appointment of coaches and administrators for next season met with full approval.

On the UEFA event I was told that nothing had happened during the previous month, albeit that after the draw for group places had been made in Llanelli we had visits from representatives of some of the participating countries. All the club had received was a pitchside banner which had been draped over a board by the home dugout. We shrugged our shoulders: there was now less than two months before the first match would start. We want our part of the festival to run smoothly and to publicise it as much as possible. The newspapers had received no copy, nor had the town's commercial concerns received

Liam Thomas & Rhys Felton

any literature or promotional material.

The following day I received some leaked correspondence. It was between the FAW and Carmarthenshire's Marketing & Tourism Manager, Huw Parsons. Ten days earlier the FAW seem to have woken up to the fact that they had forgotten to liaise with the county council and were now trying desperately to find a way to rectify matters.

The utter drivel and piffle, couched in modern day marketing jargon, being put forward from Cardiff needed many references to my dictionary to actually understand what last minute pleas

Liam Thomas & Craig Hanford

were being made. The reaction from Huw Parsons to various questionable concepts showed complete professionalism on his part. From his short replies I felt that he, like many of us, was wondering what on earth was going on. If it was not for the fact that my club were so deeply involved I would walk backwards very quickly.

Because of the uncertainty concerning our involvement in the Europa League

Alan Elias, Chris Davies & Steve Jones

play-off matches, the Players' Presentation Evening could not be held until the holiday weekend at the end of May. This meant that the number of supporters present was the lowest for some time although the players from all three teams were there in abundance.

It was an evening of appreciation, particularly from the three team managers, Peter Fearn, Steve Jones and Mark Aizlewood, who praised their respective teams for the season's work. Awards were handed out; thanks were given; cheques passed over from various fund-raising groups as the campaign drew slowly to its conclusion.

There were three Player-of-the-Year Awards made to members of the first-team. The Supporters' Club Award went to Liam Thomas; the Players' Player Award was won by Ian Hillier with the Club Award going to Craig Hanford.

Ryan Stephens & Peter Fearn

After presenting the final trophy Aize said a few words of encouragement and the evening just drifted away.

As far as the playing side were concerned that was it for 2012/13. Off the field things were already moving for the new term. We were going to lose Geoff Kellaway who was returning to his home town, Aberystwyth, for purely personal reasons. Aize had lined up five new signings, three of whom were highly experienced WPL players, while all of the other team members had committed themselves for another year.

The pitch had been transformed into what looked like a storage area for fossil fuel with not an inch of greenery to be seen. Jonathan Lewis pointed out a peg in the ground: "That is going to be the new level," he said. I was amazed as it seemed to be far higher than in the past. "It's all to do with the slope," I was told. I hope the weather holds so the work can be completed on schedule.

In the southern corner work had nearly finished on the new changing room building. Fittings were being completed for the new 'Old Gold Brassèrie' with the former Tea Hut building having disappeared. It really was going to be all change for when we return in the autumn.

Off the field there was the Twenty-First Annual General Meeting of the Welsh Premier League to attend. This year it was held in North Wales, only a couple of miles from the Connah's Quay ground.

As soon as I walked into the foyer of the St.David's Hotel in Ewloe I knew it was going to be like a gathering of an Old Boys Association. There were handshakes all round and virtually at once all of the tensions of the season seemed to evaporate. People greeted each other as long lost friends with rivalries put to one side. With a twelve team league the familiarity had started to forge friendships and it was only the folk from newly elected Rhyl who were unfamiliar to us.

Mel Thomas, the WPL record keeper, was handing out copies of his Annual Report. It was an excellent work of statistical detail and immediately my eyes found the section marked 'Disciplinary Analysis.' There, in all of its glory, were the Fair Play Award figures for the season. Of the red cards handed out in all matches we had received 21% of them. We also had the most yellow cards (76) and our penalty points total of 426 was a new WPL record. Newtown topped the poll with just 148 points.

But Mel had also noted much more. Although attendances were down (we had lost an average of thirty-one spectators per match) the figures for games played on a Friday evening had risen. For Sunday afternoon fixtures they had completely collapsed. These were discussed during the AGM and club delegates pointed out that a twelve team league was hugely unpopular with spectators but their views were not accepted by the top table.

There were a number of Agenda items which went through on the nodding of heads. Gwyn Derfel kept things moving well and it was obvious as to how he had grown into the job over the previous twelve months since taking over from John Deakin. Then came the surprise: Tony Bates had resigned from the WPL Panel which had subsequently created a vacancy. The only nomination had been our own G.O. and he was elected by acclaim.

During the afternoon the FAW had presented both the UEFA and WPL licensing certificates to a delegate from each club. These pieces of paper were the most valuable documents a club could possess for without them they could not play in Wales' Premier League.

*　　*　　*　　*　　*

Looking back over the previous twelve months has made me realise how much work actually goes into making a club like ours tick over from season to season. On many occasions I have got annoyed and frustrated with various individuals (and, no doubt, they with me) but we are all in it together.

I have little idea as to how Jeff Thomas, as our Business Director, brings in the funds to keep the club alive. As Aize says regularly: "Carmarthen have never missed paying their players." G.O. is a full-time secretary in all but name and at our weekly meetings he never ceases to surprise me with the detail needed to fulfil his functions. One piece of paper out of place and chaos can ensue.

Carmarthen Town Football Club is part of the community in more than one way. We all try to do our best and the assistance given to us from the County Council; local business leaders; club members and supporters, and even the unemployed is all accepted in the kind way it is given.

I am sure that the UEFA tournament will have survived all of its teething problems and before we know it a new season will be upon us. So far the Old Gold have played in 576 WPL matches: There will be many more.

INDEX

Presentation of the UEFA Licence

Matches Played
2012/13 season

Date	Club	H/A	Competition	Score	Scorers	Attendance
14.07.12	Barry Town	A	PSF	3 - 2	Fowler (2), Hughes	35
14.07.12	West End	A	PSF	4 - 2	L.Thomas (3) , Rees	79
21.07.12	Newport County	H	PSF	3 - 1	Hood, Jeanne, Hughes	189
28.07.12	Swansea City	H	PSF	1 - 1	Hood	182
04.08.12	Taff's Well	A	PSF	1 - 0	L. Thomas	46
11.08.12	Cwmbran Town	A	PSF	7 - 1	F'bach, Hood, Hicks, Hughes, Christopher, Co. T'mas, L. T'mas	88
18.08.12	Aberystwyth Town	H	WPL	2 - 0	Christopher, L. Thomas	407
25.08.12	Airbus Broughton	A	WPL	2 - 1	Co. Thomas, L. Thomas	191
31.08.12	Afan Lido	H	WPL	1 - 1	Christopher	413
04.09.12	Afan Lido	A	WPL	1 - 2	Hicks	323
08.09.12	Prestatyn Town	A	WPL	1 - 7	Hicks	250
15.09.12	The New Saints	H	WPL	0 - 0	--	297
22.09.12	Bala Town	A	WPL	0 - 3	--	179
29.09.12	Bangor City	H	WPL	0 - 1	--	281
05.10.12	Port Talbot Town	A	WPL	1 - 2	Jeanne	248
09.10.12	Bryntirion Athletic	A	LC	2 - 1	L. Thomas (2)	150
13.10.12	Connah's Quay	H	WPL	2 - 4	L. Thomas, Hood	255
20.10.12	Newtown	A	WPL	2 - 1	Ca. Thomas, L. Thomas	325
27.10.12	Aberystwyth Town	A	WPL	0 - 1	--	352
30.10.12	Port Talbot Town	H	LC	3 - 2	L. Thomas (2), McCreesh	147
03.11.12	Airbus Broughton	H	WPL	2 - 1	L. Thomas (2)	243
08.11.12	Llanelli	H	LC	2 - 1	Ca. Thomas, Alsop	197
17.11.12	Prestatyn Town	H	WPL	2 - 2	L. Thomas (2)	334
24.11.12	The New Saints	A	WPL	3 - 0	Fowler, Palmer, L. Thomas	224
01.12.12	Bala Town	H	WPL	1 - 1	L.Thomas	323
08.12.12	Holyhead Hotspur	A	FAW	2 - 1	L. Thomas (2)	307
15.12.12	Bangor City	A	WPL	2 - 2	Hughes, L. Thomas	418
21.12.12	Port Talbot Town	H	WPL	1 - 0	Hood	324
26.12.12	Llanelli	H	WPL	1 - 0	C. Evans	364
29.12.12	Llanelli	A	WPL	2 - 4	L. Thomas (2)	243
05.01.13	Connah's Quay	A	WPL	1 - 1	Hughes	202
12.01.13	The New Saints	N	LC	3 - 3	Hughes, Co.Thomas (2)	455
Won		on	penalties	3 - 1	Co.Thomas, L.Thomas, Hanford	
26.01.13	Bala Town	H	FAW	3 - 2	(a.e.t) L. Thomas (2), Hughes	303
02.02.13	Newtown	H	WPL	4 - 2	Kellaway (2), Doidge (2)	283
19.02.13	Taff's Well	A	F	3 - 3	L.Thomas (2), Fowler	20
23.02.13	Bangor City	H	WPL	0 - 1	--	236
02.03.13	Prestatyn Town	H	FAW	2 - 3	(a.e.t) Kellaway, Hughes	204
08.03.13	Port Talbot Town	A	WPL	0 - 1	--	310
16.03.13	Prestatyn Town	H	WPL	3 - 2	Co.T'mas, McCreesh, Ca.T'mas	205
30.03.13	The New Saints	A	WPL	0 - 3	--	312
06.04.13	Airbus Broughton	H	WPL	1 - 0	Co. Thomas	167
09.04.13	Airbus Broughton	A	WPL	0 - 2	--	181
13.04.13	Bangor City	A	WPL	0 - 2	--	472
16.04.13	The New Saints	H	WPL	0 - 1	--	297
20.04.13	Port Talbot Town	H	WPL	0 - 0	--	305
27.04.13	Prestatyn Town	A	WPL	1 - 2	Kellaway	233
11.05.13	Port Talbot Town	A	EPO	0 - 1	--	410

Player Record

2012/13 season

Name	Total Played	Total Sub	Total Goals	WPL Played	WPL Sub	WPL Goals	Cup/ EPO Played	Cup/ EPO Sub	Cup/ EPO Goals
Corey Thomas	34	4	5	28	3	3	6	1	2
Craig Hanford	34	0	0	27	0	0	7	0	0
Steven Cann	31	0	0	24	0	0	7	0	0
Liam Thomas	30	5	21	24	4	13	6	1	8
Ian Hillier	30	5	0	23	4	0	7	1	0
Paul Fowler	29	4	1	23	4	1	6	0	0
Matthew Rees	28	3	0	23	3	0	5	0	0
Liam McCreesh	28	2	2	23	1	1	5	1	1
Tim Hicks	25	7	2	22	5	2	3	2	0
Nicky Palmer	22	3	1	17	3	1	5	0	0
Carl Evans	22	2	1	18	2	1	4	0	0
Casey Thomas	19	10	3	13	8	2	6	2	1
Craig Hughes	12	5	5	8	4	2	4	1	3
Luke Cummings	12	2	0	8	2	0	4	0	0
Geoff Kellaway	12	0	4	11	0	3	1	0	1
Neil Smothers	10	4	0	8	3	0	2	1	0
Iestyn Evans	7	5	0	4	3	0	3	2	0
Christian Doidge	6	8	2	5	7	2	1	1	0
Kerry Nicholas	5	0	0	4	0	0	1	0	0
Sam Wilson	1	9	0	1	6	0	0	3	0
Namir Queni	1	0	0	1	0	0	0	0	0
Finton O'Brien	0	1	0	0	1	0	0	0	0
Players no longer with Club									
Jonathan Hood	14	8	2	12	4	2	2	4	0
Leon Jeanne	6	2	1	6	1	1	0	1	0
Danny Thomas	5	5	0	4	5	0	1	0	0
Jack Christopher	5	1	2	5	1	2	0	0	0
Scott Quigley	4	0	0	4	0	0	0	0	0
Julian Alsop	3	2	1	2	2	0	1	0	1
Rhys Wilson	3	0	0	3	0	0	0	0	0
Anth. Finselbach	2	0	0	1	0	0	1	0	0
Kyle Graves	0	2	0	0	1	0	0	1	0

Carmarthen Town Current Players

Correct to end 2012/13 season

WPL (only)	Starts	Sub	Goals
Tim Hicks	180	70	52
Paul Fowler	149	5	18
Neil Smothers	131	23	4
Nicky Palmer	106	20	11
Corey Thomas	62	21	7
Craig Hanford	52	1	-
Craig Hughes	44	9	14
Liam Thomas	24	4	13
Steve Cann	24	-	-
Ian Hillier	23	4	-
Matthew Rees	23	3	-
Liam McCreesh	23	1	1
Carl Evans	18	2	1
Casey Thomas	13	8	2
Geoff Kellaway	11	-	3
Luke Cummings	8	2	-
Christian Doidge	5	7	2
Iestyn Evans	4	3	-
Kerry Nicholas	4	-	-
Sam Wilson	1	6	-
Namir Queni	1	-	-
Finton O'Brien	-	1	-

WPL Appearances

Correct to end 2012/13 season (Qualification 25 games)

Player	Appearances	Player	Appearances
David Barnhouse	183	David Morgan	45
Dean Rossiter	182	Gavin Rees	45
Tim Hicks	180	Craig Evans	45
Nathan Cotterall	165	Lee Bevan	45
Paul Fowler	149	Craig Hughes	44
Sacha Walters	138	Kieran Howard	43
Wyn Thomas	132	Kaid Mohamed	43
Neil Smothers	131	Chris Summers	42
Mark Dodds	127	Nicky Burke	42
Neil Thomas	123	Ceri Williams	41
Wayne Jones	121	Dale Griffiths	41
Danny Thomas	116	Rhodri Jones	41
Robert Fitzgerald	107	Leigh De-Vulgt	41
Nicky Palmer	106	Richard Thomas	40
Richard Hughes	105	Malcolm Vaughan	38
Chris Thomas	104	Owen Thomas	37
Ryan Nicholls	101	Richard Carter	37
Stephen Evans	96	Paul Burrows	36
Neil O'Brien	93	Richard Kennedy	35
Sion Meredith	89	Jack Christopher	35
Shaun Chapple	73	Lee Jones	34
Matthew Cable	71	Paul Walker	34
Liam Hancock	66	Colin Loss	32
Tony Pennock	66	Gregg Coombes	32
Richard Parker	62	Colin Pascoe	31
Corey Thomas	62	Tom Ramasut	30
Mike Lewis	60	Jamal Easter	30
Martyn Giles	60	Craig Lima	30
Mark Delaney	58	Terry Evans	30
Simon Rocke	56	Geraint Passmore	29
Luke Hardy	56	Steven Williams	29
Nick Harrhy	52	Chris Miller	28
Craig Hanford	52	Cledan Davies	28
Jon Keaveney	49	Phillip Davidson	27
Gary Lloyd	48	Stuart Roberts	27
Dale Price	47	Andrew York	27
Deryn Brace	46	Carl Harris	26
Kevin A-Evans	46	Andrew Delve	25
Nigel Nicholas	46		

Carmarthen Town WPL Goalscorers

(Qualification 10 goals) Correct to end 2012/13 season

Danny Thomas	56
Tim Hicks	52
Ryan Nicholls	34
Richard Parker	28
Sacha Walters	28
Chris Summers	27
Nathan Cotterrall	24
Jonathan Keaveney	21
Kaid Mohamed	19
Paul Fowler	18
Sion Meredith	15
Craig Hughes	14
Liam Thomas	13
Mattie Davies	13
Nick Harrhy	13
Simon Jones	12
Ceri Williams	12
Kevin Aherne-Evans	12
Chris Thomas	12
Mark Dodds	12
Matthew Delicate	11
Jamal Easter	11
Paul Burrows	11
Nicky Palmer	11
Wyn Thomas	11
Craig Lima	10
Wayne Jones	10

WHO'S WHO AT RICHMOND PARK

President / Business Director : Jeff Thomas

Chairman : Neil Alexander

Secretary / Football Director / Safeguarding Officer / Programme Editor : Gareth Jones

Finance Director / Security Officer : Anthony Parnell

Community Director / Club Shop : Paul Ashley-Jones

Director of Communications : Chris Harte

Matchday Secretary / Webmaster : Huw Davies

Social Club Committee Chairman : Colin Payne

Stadium Facilities Manager / Safety Officer : Jonathan Lewis

Chief Steward : Andrew Thomas

Vice Presidents / Season Tickets : Clive Thomas

Management Committee : As above plus Keiran Davies, Rhys Felton, Peter Hughes-Griffiths, Roger Hunt, Steve Jones

Club Brassèrie / Ladies' Committee : Cordelia Evans (chair), Diane Davies, Wendy Davies, Cheryl Jenkins, Jan Payne, Eirlys Thomas, Jenny Williams, Olga Williams.

Assistant Secretary : vacant

Financial Advisor : Alan Dodd

Supporters' Liaison : Rhys Felton

Club Shop Manager : Celia Kirkby

Licensing Officer / Matchday Reporter : John Collyer

Programme Contributors : Alun Charles, Alan Latham

Match Posters : Alun Williams

Public Address Announcers : Geraint Hughes, Peter Hughes-Griffiths

Stadium Maintenance : Willy Thomas, John Davidson, Mike Stacey

Steward : Antony Powell

Security Officer : Malcolm Williams

Turnstile Operators : Clive Evans, Paul Evans, Pam Davies (Senior Academy)

Club Chef : Mark Hannington

Community Centre Manager : Michelle Hopkins

Club Solicitor : Edward Friend

First Team / Academy Manager : Mark Aizlewood

First Team Coach : Neil Smothers

Assistant Coach / Academy Administrator : Keiran Davies

Goalkeeping Coach : Rob Thomas

Equipment Manager : Gareth Davies

Physiotherapists : Gary Morris, Matthew Lewis

Club Doctor : Llinos Roberts

Reserve Team Manager : Steve Jones

Reserve Team Assistant Manager : Chris Davies

Reserve Team Goalkeeping Coach : Robert Brooks

Reserve Team Physiotherapist : Alan Elias

Senior Academy Team Coach : Peter Fearn

Senior Academy Coach / Administrator : Sean Cresser

Senior Academy Coaches : Lyn Brodrick, Ryan Stephens

Junior Academy Coaches : Serge Bonandrini, Owain Thomas, Damon Howells

Schools Tournament : Emlyn Schiavone

*OK! Who nicked
the Tea Bar?*

Early pitch work

*Jonathan Lewis working
on the pitch*

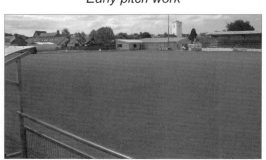

Before seeding

Don't drop the pen, Steve!

Iestyn Evans' Cap

Sam Wilson's Cap

Jody Thomas & Steve 'Gas'

Trinity Students

*Jeff Thomas &
Jonathan Edwards M.P.*

The UEFA Licence

JACK HARDING'S FOOTBALL CAREER
(1920-1939)

Once he had settled back into civilian life and set up home with his new wife May, Jack soon got involved with St.Peter's FC. This church based club, whose colours were royal blue, had to play a bulk of their matches away from home. This was due to the Town Council only allowing them five Saturdays a year on the New King George Field.

The argument put forward by the Town Councillors against having more football matches was: "That the Association players cause more damage to the pitch than the rugby players." This illogical thinking had a lot to do with the snobbishness of the time towards the oval ball game.

Jack played around twenty-seven games each year and all went well until an incident towards the end of the 1924/25 season. In late March, in a home fixture against Kilgetty, Jack was sent off for committing a foul tackle. The club's committee met three days later to consider the incident.

Jack was furious at the dismissal and addressed the gathering saying: "I wish to bring forward a number of witnesses to prove I did not commit a foul." His offer was not required as the committee decided to take no further action.

It is obvious that Jack was unhappy not to be completely exonerated and left the club a few weeks later. Had he wanted to continue playing on the eastern side of town he could have chosen to join either Carmarthen Harlequins, St.Peter's Church House or Carmarthen Celtic football clubs. Instead he chose to join the Pensarn based Quay Rovers.

The first season of the Mond Cup was 1925/26 and within three years the organisers invited Quay Rovers to participate. They did not have much success in either this competition or any other matches. Pitches were hard to find and when any did become available the rent required (normally from publican owners) was beyond the clubs' means.

Jack was a born organiser and in the summer of 1930, with the agreement of his committee, he approached the St.Peter's chairman, William Baker, to see what they thought about an amalgamation. Jack's original idea was to call the new club Carmarthen United. Finding that he had little support for the name he went for his second choice, St.Peter's Rovers. This was unanimously supported by all attending the joint meeting which approved the merger. The chosen colours would be black and white striped jerseys.

The new ground for the club was Carmarthen Park. With Jack now Assistant Secretary he was able to persuade the rest of his committee to affiliate the club to the Llanelli Football Association as they now had a quality venue to go with their new status. An overture from the Carmarthenshire Football League was rejected and the club joined the Llanelli & District Football League.

By the start of the 1931/32 season Jack had become the team's selector and by the beginning of the following season he had been elected club chairman. The 1933/34 season was full of success which culminated in the winning of the Mond Cup. Later in 1934, Jack handed over the chairman's position to Charles Lloyd and then became the team manager.

Before then Jack had continued playing. In the merged club's first match, in September 1930, he had scored the seventh goal in the 9-0 away victory at Kidwelly. He finished the season with four goals in twenty-seven appearances.

He did better in 1931/32 doubling his tally to eight goals in twenty-eight games, which included a brace in the 6-1 home win against Lampeter College in late October. He only scored once more in the next two seasons before hanging up his boots to concentrate on management.

Under Jack's guiding hand the Mond Cup was won again in 1934/35. The team were successful in eighteen of their matches, scoring 89 goals of which Harry Trumper got 34 and Benny Elias 25. The trophy was formally handed over to the captain Ben Jones at a 'smoking concert' held at The Golden Lion Hotel, Lammas Street at the end of the season.

For their 1935/36 home matches the club had acquired a lease to use the Buffalo Bill Fields in Johnstown. This brought stability to the club and allowed Jack to organise very basic training sessions. Usually, to keep fit, the players would walk briskly around a street circuit but once Jack got things organised they also took part in gymnastics. On the playing side the season saw only sixteen wins from thirty-four games, which included a Mond Cup semi-final defeat 5-2 away at Ponthenry Welfare following a home 1-1 draw.

The 1936/37 season started badly with a heavy defeat away at Haverfordwest. This saw Jack make a number of changes to his team but it did not stop a first round Mond Cup defeat 4-3 away to Burry Port. However, one interesting point to note was that the 3-3 draw away to Briton Ferry "created a new ground record attendance." The winter was so bad that the St.Peter's secretary, Thomas Twigg, noted: "Our match in Lampeter, against the College (a 5-3 defeat) was played in a blizzard." Four weeks later, in the return fixture (lost 2-1) he noted: "The conditions were atrocious."

During the summer the committee decided to move home yet again. From now, until the club folded with the advent of war, St.Peter's Rovers played at Parc Hinds in Priory Street. The move proved successful on the field with

a Llanelli & District League championship and a Mond Cup semi-final appearance (a 2-1 defeat against Pontyates United). At the annual 'smoking concert' Jack was presented with two gifts from the club members in appreciation of his efforts. He received an unplucked goose and a box of one hundred cigarettes. The records do not show if the club was in financial difficulty but in what seems an unusual move Jack paid the year's affiliation fee of three shillings and nine pence (19p) "to the Welsh Football Association."

The last season before the war saw the club finish runners up in the league and they were once again Mond Cup finalists. The Cup occupied a number of Saturdays as the quarter-final against Cross Hands went to two replays (1-1, 1-1, 3-0) before Trimsaran were beaten 2-1 in the semi-final. Pontyates were again victorious in the final, this time 2-0.

Jack finished his managerial career with some notable victories to his name. St.Clears had been beaten away 12-2; Gorsddu (Gorslas) 10-0 and 7-3; Cross Hands 8-1 and Ponyberem 7-0. On the other side of the coin an 11-0 home defeat to Llanelli and a 7-2 loss at Haverfordwest were not matches he would have remembered fondly.

After the war, in 1946, Jack and others tried to form a Carmarthen Athletic side but the club never established itself. Then, in 1950, came the advent of the club which we know today.

Canolfan Gymunedol / Community Centre

C.P.D.Tref Caerfyrddin
Carmarthen Town A.F.C.

ROOMS AVAILABLE FOR HIRE

Meetings; Parties; Group Gatherings; Club Venues;
Regular Events; One-Off Occasions

• FULLY AIR CONDITIONED •
• FULLY LICENSED BAR FACILITIES •
• LIVE COVERAGE OF PREMIER LEAGUE
& EUROPEAN MATCHES •

Cyswllt / Contact : **Michelle Hopkins 07581 238352**
neu / or **Mark Hannington 07929 509539**

ebost / email : **markfootieclub@hotmail.com**

174